BORGES IN/AND/ON FILM

Edgardo Cozarinsky

BORGES IN/AND/ON FILM

Translated by Gloria Waldman and Ronald Christ

Lumen Books

Excerpts from this translation have appeared, in different form, in the magazines *Sight and Sound*, *October*, *Nimrod*, and *SITES*, as well as in *Argentine Cinema* (Toronto, 1986).

© *1988 Lumen Inc. Translation* © *1988 Ronald Christ, world rights in English reserved.*
ISBN 0-930829-08-5

Lumen Books are produced by Lumen Inc., a tax-exempt, non-profit organization. This publication is made possible, in part, with public funds from the New York State Council on the Arts, the National Endowment for the Arts, and with private contributions.

Lumen Books
446 West 20 Street
New York, NY 10011

Published in Spain as *Borges en/y/sobre cine*. © 1980 Edgardo Cozarinsky.
© 1981 Editorial Fundamentos.

Contents

Prologue by Adolfo Bioy-Casares 1
Foreword by Edgardo Cozarinsky 3
A Note on the Translation 5

Partial Enchantments of Narrative.................... 9

Borges on Film
  Reviews
    FILMS (*Der Mörder Dimitri Karamasoff,
      City Lights, Morocco*) 23
    STREET SCENE................................. 27
    THE INFORMER 30
    TWO FILMS (*Crime and Punishment,
      The Thirty-nine Steps*) 33
    THE PETRIFIED FOREST 35
    WELLS THE VISIONARY (*Things to Come*) 37
    FILM AND THEATRE........................... 40
    TWO FILMS (*Sabotage, Los muchachos
      de antes no usaban gomina*) 44
    LA FUGA...................................... 47
    GREEN PASTURES 49
    THE ROAD BACK 51
    PRISIONEROS DE LA TIERRA 53
    AN OVERWHELMING FILM (*Citizen Kane*) 55
    DR. JEKYLL AND MR. HYDE TRANSFORMED ... 57
    TWO FILMS (*Now Voyager, Nightmare*)............ 59
    ON DUBBING.................................. 62
    FIVE BRIEF ITEMS............................. 65

  A Prologue....................................... 69
  Two Synopses of Films............................ 72

Film on Borges
  Adventures of the Text
    A Source for Exegetes........................... 77
    A Source for Cinéastes 87
  Versions and Perversions............................ 93

Prologue

As enjoyable as it is useful, this admirable book presented to us by Edgardo Cozarinsky brings back memories of the earliest years of my friendship with Borges. In those days, we used to talk a lot about books and films (with a special bias for the plots: plots of novels, short stories, films, and even poems, such as those by Victor Hugo and Robert Browning). Film was always an important art for Borges. I would venture to say that if he had composed a list of the works that moved him most at the time, we would find more than a few films included. Nevertheless, he once said to me: "At the movies, we're all readers of Madame Delly."[1] If that assertion implied a certain reservation, Borges's enthusiasm for films was unbridled by it. At its worst, the remark might be interpreted as a judgment on the films already made, not the ones still possible. But I take the remark essentially as an indication of Borges's capacity to see things quickly in a new, unexpected, and realistic way, as well as of his capacity for turning himself, at any moment, into a sort of devil's advocate.

Perhaps at this point I should quote a young fellow's remark that I once overheard in a bookstore on the Boulevard Saint Michel: "Borges's opinions annoy me twice over. First, when I find them arbitrary; second, when I find them right."

Adolfo Bioy-Casares

---

[1] Pen-name of Marie (1875-1947) and Frédèric (1876-1949) Petitjean de la Rosière, sister and brother whose romantic fiction was immensely popular with female readers in the first half of this century. Starting with *Une femme supérieure* in 1907, some hundred titles had appeared under their common signature by 1941. Delly's popularity was extraordinary throughout Latin America, and the novels are regarded as the main influence on Corín Tellado. In France today, pocket reprints of the books run to 100,000 copies.

Foreword

In 1935, when he published the original prologue to his *Universal History of Infamy*, Borges admitted that his first exercises in fiction derived from the films of von Sternberg. In 1940, when he published his *Anthology of Fantastic Literature* (compiled with Adolfo Bioy-Casares and Silvina Ocampo and serving as a nondiscursive manifesto, proceeding by example, for the literary choices illustrated by their later work), one of the seven lines giving information about Borges announced: "He writes, in vain, scripts for films. . . ."

Borges's relationship with film has been as labyrinthine and surprising as his characters' relation to time, and this book attempts to inventory, on a necessarily provisional basis, the numerous, even contradictory aspects of that relationship. Consequently, the central section comprises those reviews of individual films as well as the essays on various aspects of cinematographic language that Borges published in the Argentine literary magazine SUR between 1931 and 1944. These reviews, however, are merely the most explicit among many references to film scattered throughout Borges's splendidly fragmentary and only seemingly discontinuous "text"—to use that term, since he disdained the label *oeuvre*. In that reiterating text, one can recognize not only a series of attitudes toward film, but also ideas on all narrative practice, options dramatized in the writing of a story and already implicit in Borges's treatment of movies. Such a recognition is what I have attempted in my introductory essay. In the last section of the book, I track down—with less erudition than humor, and greater curiosity about the unpredictable results than any qualms about fidelity—Borges's almost parodic impact on critics and filmmakers (sometimes one and the same person) who have quoted him, and on the films that have adapted his stories and interpreted his original plots for movies. Predictably, the resulting book incorporates all these materials in a nonlinear fashion, respecting, instead, their diversity and allowing them to radiate in different directions from a common center.

I have been able to edit and compile all this material thanks to the generosity and patience of Adolfo Bioy-Casares and Alberto

Tabbia as well as the good will of Carlos Clarens, Jorge Dana, Eduardo de Gregorio, Bernard Eisenschitz, Paulina and Guilermo Fernández Jurado, Hugo Santiago, Roberto "Dodi" Scheuer, and Emilio Soler. My gratitude to them all.

While the 1981 Spanish edition was the first to respect the title I orginally chose for my book, this present edition not only "corrects, augments, and updates" the book entitled *Borges y el cine*, which disappeared in Argentina in 1974; this edition also includes material that had only appeared in the Italian edition (Il Formichiere, 1978) and other material added to the French edition (Albatros, 1979) and to various other editions since then. I think Borges might have been pleased by the idea of a book whose different editions do not coincide, either in title or in content.

Edgardo Cozarinsky
Paris, June 1980

A Footnote for the English-language Edition

This belated publication in English should be attributed to the generosity and perseverance of Ronald Christ, who overcame my reluctance to look over these notes. Not completely, though: I have not tried to keep track of all the allusions to Borges in the films of these last years, let alone those in film criticism. I gladly entrust that task to younger, more curious academic sleuths. Nevertheless, in order to keep each edition of the book somehow different from the previous ones, there are some minute additions of my own as well as a whole new section from the Master: "*Cinco breves noticias*" ("*Five Brief Items*"), which were discovered by the poet Alberto Vila Ortiz in a 1933 issue of the magazine *Selección*. Sent by him to María Esther Vázquez, these *noticias* were reprinted in the Buenos Aires newspaper *La Nación* on March 1, 1987. Both writers are to be thanked for bringing to light these occasional pieces, which, however minor, are not worth the oblivion Borges wished for them.

Paris, September 1987

A Note on the Translation

When I asked Borges about his writings on films—it was 1976, in Orono, Maine—he replied: "Look here, they're not writings. Those are mere scratchings. And they deserve to be forgotten." No one has agreed with his signature remark and certainly not Victoria Ocampo, who first commissioned them for her magazine SUR and later published them in *Borges y el cine* by Edgardo Cozarinsky. I spoke with her about translating the book in collaboration with Gloria Waldman, and she gave me an early copy, inscribed: "This is my answer to Borges who said I was not interested in cinema." Dismissal from the great writer on the one hand, revenge from the formidable publisher on the other (from the woman who saw two, three movies a day, walking out on many of them, some before the opening credits were over). Not very auspicious for the publication, especially when it didn't even bear the name with which its author had baptized it. No wonder, then, that this is the book that "disappeared," in Argentina, as Cozarinsky says.

And it almost disappeared in English too. With a twelve-year history, nearly as populous as a Keystone Kops chase (and some incidents nearly as grave), Cozarinsky's book finally makes its appearance in our language, and a few words need to be said about its translation. The "scratchings" that Borges committed in these early pages are often rhetorical in a formal, patterned way, and we have tried to preserve the effect of these patterns, much condemned by the later Borges and some of his translators. He came, he said, to prefer "straightforward" writing, and too much of contemporary English prose shares the preference; but he had been a writer of intelligible mazes, rhetorical paths, long before he appeared to be trying on a Danish-modern style. We have also listened to his insistent religious imagery, which puts the ephemera of the screen in the perspective of the Last Things. (We tried turning a deaf ear to the one murmur of anti-Semitism, but it is there for anyone who cares to hear it.)

More specifically, we have translated quotations from Borges's other writings ourselves, except in rare instances where the work may be better known in an existing English version. With Borges's own translated citations, most often from English, we have followed the original where that seemed to make no difference to the sense or appended the original in a footnote. But, as in the case of his essay on H. G. Wells's *Things to Come*, where he effectively alters the original, we have added notes. Most readers will want to ignore these footnotes, which also supply explanatory data on occasion, and we urge them to do so; but for those with a curiosity about Borges's games with texts, his faulty and fabulous quoting from memory, for those, perhaps, with an interest more literary than cinematic, these notes may serve. They make no claim to scholarly thoroughness. That would be out of place in a growing assemblage. As for Borges's divergences from the facts of the films he writes about—*Battleship Potemkin* offers a good example—we have passed over them in silence. (When I asked Borges certain questions about the essays, he told me he couldn't recall the answers, he feigned not even remembering having written the pieces. Then he added contentedly: "That's the trouble with American authors: they think they have to know everything before they write a book.") These numbered footnotes from the translators will be found at the end of each section or review; Borges's and Cozarinsky's notes appear at the foot of the page with an asterisk.

References to foreign movies are kept in the original language except when the title of their English-language release is added or when a translation is supplied because it seemed necessary to a full understanding of the passage.

For assisting us, we owe greatest thanks to Edgardo Cozarinsky, who answered so many questions, and Helen R. Lane, who meticulously encouraged us with advice on parts of the translation. In addition, we want to thank Kieran Bartley, Dennis Dollens, Robin Orlandi, Elizabeth Schneider, and William Vesterman for their assistance, and to acknoweldge, with gratitude, the support of the Rutgers University Research Council. All that is rewarding in this book comes from its several authors; any imperfections in the translation are our contribution.

When I discussed this work with Borges—in 1976, in Orono, Maine—I suggested that translating all too often is the art of imperfecting. He smiled his laugh and replied: "And that's true of literature also, no?"

R.C.
New York, 1988

PARTIAL ENCHANTMENTS OF NARRATIVE

Writers have always wanted to create cinema on the blank page: to arrange all the elements and let thought roam among them.

Jean-Luc Godard
Interviewed in *Cahiers du Cinema* 171, October 1965

1

Film—an *idea* of film, really—recurs in Borges's writing linked to the practice of narration, even to the possibility of attempting narration. Films also appear as reading matter, one among the countless motives for reflection lavished on us by the universe. The examples offered to Borges by films illustrate widely disparate themes: the hilarious response of a Buenos Aires audience to some scenes from *Hallelujah* and *Underworld* provoked his bitter commentary on "Our Impossibilities" (an article dating from 1931 and included in *Discusión* the following year but eliminated from the 1957 edition); von Sternberg gave him the chance to confirm a hypothesis about the workings of all story telling ("The Postulation of Reality" and "Narrative Art and Magic," both included in *Discusión);* Joan Crawford made an appearance in the second of these essays and Miriam Hopkins in "History of Eternity" from the volume of the same title; "the impetuous film *Hallelujah"* furnished one of the many results of bringing blacks to America that Borges enumerates in *Universal History of Infamy;* the modest translator Edward William Lane provided a basis for Borges's comparison with Hollywood's then rigid censorship code ("The Translators of the 1001 Nights," *History of Eternity*).

During the 1920s and '30s, Borges saw the mere diffusion of images by means of film as an incalculable enrichment of life, perhaps because he knew how to recognize in those images, even though they were fictitious—or, above all, *because* they were fictitious?—signs of a broader context. In a digression, subsequently deleted when he revised *Discusión,* Borges refers in his 1929 essay "The Other Whitman" to the lack of communication between inhabitants of "the diverse Americas," and he proceeds to venture an opinion: it is "a lack of communication that films, with their direct presentation of destinies and their no less direct presentation of wills, tend to overcome." This catalogue of references could be extended effortlessly, but its sole importance is to establish the degree to which films were a habit for the young Borges, an accessible repertoire of allusions, which he consulted as frequently as the *Encyclopedia Britannica* or unpublished reality.

At that time, film represented to Borges the image of literature (or history or philosophy) as a single text fragmented into countless, even contradictory passages, which neither individually represented that text nor in combination exhausted it. With even greater ease than in those prestigious disciplines, this notion could come to life in the films Borges frequented and quoted from, with diminishing regularity after 1940: a cinema that in spite of Eisenstein and Welles could still seem an art unfettered by too many big names, a cinema that was, above all else, free of bibliographies and academies. Allardyce Nicoll, whose *Film and Theatre* (1936) Borges dismissed as an exercise in pedantry, seemed "well versed in libraries, erudite in card catalogues, sovereign in files," but "nearly illiterate in box-offices. . . ."

In this cinematic realm, many obscure narrators practiced the "differing intonation of a few metaphors" ("The Sphere of Pascal," *Other Inquisitions)* whose history may be the history of the universe. "I think nowadays, while literary men seem to have neglected their epic duties, the epic has been saved for us, strangely enough, by the Westerns," Borges told Ronald Christ in an interview published in *The Paris Review* 40 (Winter/Spring 1967). "During this century," he said, "the epic tradition has been saved for the world by, of all places, Hollywood." If Hollywood really was able to compile a film-text, both craftsmanlike and collective, as well as bearing comparison to the ancient sagas, then Borges's predilection for that text is, *horribile dictu,* sophisticated. In order to belittle the films that von Sternberg composed around Marlene Dietrich, Borges repeatedly defends von Sternberg's earlier action films; and, in the interview with Christ, he recalls that "when I saw the first gangster films of von Sternberg I remember that when there was anything epic about them—I mean Chicago gangsters dying bravely—well, I felt that my eyes were full of tears." But von Sternberg was neither Wellman nor Hawks nor Walsh—figures who, with greater credibility, might embody a cinematic skald. Obviously, Borges felt attracted by the stylization that von Sternberg imposed on his gangland characters, settings, and conventions, whose usual violence is less elliptical, less ironic than in films like *Underworld* or *The Docks of New York*.

It is no accident that von Sternberg is the only film director whom Borges assiduously refers to or that those references appear in his early studies of narrative technique included in *Discusión* as well as in the 1935 prologue to the *Universal History of Infamy*, where the epic invocation turns into an exercise of verbal legerdemain. In the 1954 prologue to that book, Borges writes: "Scaffolds and pirates populate it, and the word *infamy* blares in the title; but, behind all the tumult, there is nothing. The book is nothing more than appearance, nothing more than a surface of images, and for that very reason it may prove pleasurable." Films, of course, *are* that surface of images, and nothing can be found behind the words of any literary work; but to admit and flaunt one's working against the referential function of language is as skeptical and cultivated an attitude as nostalgia for epic or disdain for romantic individualism.

2

Less ascetic than Valéry, Borges put his distrust of the novel into practice. His impatience with mere length is well known: "It is an impoverishing and laborious extravagance to create long books, to extend into 500 pages an idea whose perfect oral expression takes a few minutes. A better procedure is to pretend that these books already exist and to offer a summary, a commentary" (Prologue to *The Garden of the Forking Paths*). Such boldness destroys the very possibility of even approaching a genre that, in order to develop a character and to proportion its episodes, requires a necessarily unhurried orchestration of specific circumstances and trivial information. Borges has also explained that Hawthorne's talent lent itself more to the short story than to the novel because he preferred to start from situations rather than from characters: "Hawthorne first imagined a situation, perhaps involuntarily, and afterward looked for characters to embody it. I am not a novelist, but I suspect that no novelist has proceeded in that way. . . . That method may produce, or permit, admirable short stories in which, because of their brevity, the plot is more visible than the characters; but it cannot produce admirable novels, in which the overall form (if there is any) is only visible at the end and in which a single poorly imagined character may contaminate with unreality all those characters who surround him" ("Nathaniel Hawthorne," *Other Inquisitions*).

So, then: distrust of the scale demanded by the novel and esteem for a format ("summary," "commentary") that makes "overall form" visible. As an expression of flexible disdain, of willingness to allow for occasional greatness in the practice of what he considers an erroneous genre, that phrase "if there is any" belongs to the same family as Valéry's most categorical observations. But the interesting thing about this apathy is that it does not suppose a rejection of narrative. In fact, a summary analysis of the most distinguishing characteristics in Borges's "fiction" reveals its undisguised narrative quality. The text may be a review of nonexistent literary works ("The Approach to Almotasim," "An Examination of the Works of Herbert Quain"), the exposition of apocryphal theories ("Three Versions of Judas," "The Theologians"), a report about an invented reality ("The Babylonian Lottery," "The Library of Babel"), even the connecting of probable episodes by means of a fictitious link ("History of the Warrior and the Captive," "Averroes's Search"). No matter. The less those texts respond to the accepted statutes of fiction, the more strongly they display the narrative process, which directs a *mise-en-scène* whose purpose is neither mimetic nor representational but intellectual: to arouse pleasure in the recognition of that "overall form," a recognition customarily postponed by the novel.

"The Wall and the Books," "Coleridge's Dream," "The Meeting in a Dream," and "The Modesty of History" are usually read as essays because they are included in a volume that announces itself as a collection of essays: *Other Inquisitions*. The book's real nature is a series of narrative exercises, operations that renew the workings of narrative on philosophical ideas, historical documents, and literary figures. Similarly, "History of the Warrior and Captive" or "Averroes's Search" appear in *The Aleph* and therefore are read as "fictions." Borges's categories of narrative do not discriminate between fiction and nonfiction. The only purpose of these categories is to exhibit the inherent qualities of narrative and essayistic discourse: to unearth a design that rescues the mere telling from chaos and makes an illusion of the cosmos possible. Fiction triumphs. Tlön captures and supplants the real universe with the illusion of order: "How can one not submit to Tlön, to the minute and vast evidence of an ordered planet? It is useless to answer that reality is also ordered. Perhaps it is, but in accordance with divine laws—I translate: with inhuman laws—that we never really perceive. Tlön will be a labyrinth, but a labyrinth planned by men, a labyrinth destined to be deciphered by men" ("Tlön, Uqbar, Orbis Tertius," *The Garden of the Forking Paths*).

3

Looking back after twenty years, Borges pronounced judgment on his first stories: "They are the irresponsible game of a timid man who did not dare to write stories and so amused himself by falsifying and betraying (sometimes without esthetic justification) other writers' stories" (Prologue to the 1954 edition of the *Universal History of Infamy*). *To falsify, to betray*—those verbs shock with their criminal connotations. Yet they apply to the transmission of every story, from the traditional tale and gossip to any projected novel being transformed into a written text. All narrative proceeds by repetitions and modifications of a *pre*-text, which it nullifies. Those "ambiguous games" that Borges mentions in his prologue quoted above are especially revealing because they reject the invention of anecdote, choosing to explore, instead, the various possibilities of narrative, even the mutually exclusive possibilities. In order to overcome his declared timidity, Borges both disguises and exhibits his own devices.

How did Borges view those games at the time he wrote them? In his prologue to the first edition, Borges says: "They derived, I believe, from my re-reading of Stevenson and Chesterton, and even from the first films of von Sternberg, and perhaps from a certain biography of Evaristo Carriego. They abuse some procedures: random enumeration, abrupt shifts in continuity, reduction of a man's entire life to two or three scenes." This enumeration of sources and methods, by contrast, is not random. In fact, examining his examples enables us to define the context Borges discovered for his idea of film.

In Stevenson, even in Chesterton, Borges admires a capacity for verbal *mise-en-scène*:

The threads of a story come from time to time together and make a picture in the web; the characters fall from time to time into some attitude to each other or to nature, which stamps the story home like an illustration. Crusoe recoiling from the footprint, Achilles shouting over against the Trojans, Ulysses bending the great bow, Christian running with his fingers in his ears, these are each culminating moments in the legend, and each has been printed on the mind's eye forever. Other things we may forget; we may forget the words, although they are beautiful; we may forget the author's comment although perhaps it was ingenious and true; but these epoch-making scenes, which put the last mark of truth upon a story and fill up, at one blow, our capacity for sympathetic pleasure, we so adopt into the very bosom of our mind that neither time nor tide can efface or weaken the impression. This, then, is the plastic part of literature: to embody character, thought or emotion in some act or attitude that shall be remarkably striking to the mind's eye.
(Stevenson, "A Gossip on Romance," *Memories and Portraits*, 1887).

Appreciation of verbal *mise-en-scène*, which Stevenson calls "the plastic part of literature," appears at a particular point in the evolution of narrative during the second half of the nineteenth century: after the inauguration of rigorous discipline by Flaubert; coincident with Henry James's early mastery in controlling points of view and alternating between "panorama" and "scene"; immediately before the consecration of these devices as technique in James's subsequent work as well as in the works of Conrad, Ford Maddox Ford, and the Joyce of "The Dead." Once systematized by Percy Lubbock in *The Craft of Fiction* and before languishing in the universities until it died out, this tradition provided the basis for the New Critics' best work in the study of fiction.

In "The Postulation of Reality," which appears in *Discusión,* Borges refers to these verbal, defining, and definitive images as "circumstantial invention," the third and most difficult as well as most efficient among the methods by which novelists can impose their subtle authority on the reader. He illustrates the method, magnanimously, with an example from *La gloria de Don Ramiro*[2] and adds: "I have quoted a short, linear example, but I know of expanded works—Wells's rigorously imaginative novels, Defoe's exasperatingly true-to-life ones—that use no other technique than incorporating or serializing those laconic details into a lengthy development. I assert the same thing about Josef von Sternberg's cinematographic novels, which are also made up of significant moments. It is an admirable and difficult method, but its general application makes it less strictly literary than the two previous ones." (This quotation comes from the 1957 edition of *Discussion*; the original 1932 edition reads: "cinematic, ocular novels.")

4

What can a writer do with the novelist's tools if his own intellectual habits and work with language predispose him to writing short stories and brief, intense texts? If he is also intolerant of the novel's unavoidable long stretches? Instead of finding privileged moments in the course of narrating, is it possible for him to depart from an ordering of those "significant moments" and to omit the connective tissue that should bind them together? Or, going even further, will he be able with those isolated images—so memorable within a narrative of a certain length—to conjure up phantasmagorically the absent narration that is their "lengthy development"? *Evaristo Carriego* proposes an answer.

Comparable only to Nabokov's *Nikolai Gogol* as an example of the absorption of one literary figure by another (even though the minor stature of Carriego makes the process more obvious), Borges's 1930 book on Carriego—with its discreet "betraying" and "falsifying" of another's story that scarcely serves as a pretext—is also his first approach toward that "fiction" from which a particular timidity had held him back. At several points, Borges declares his hesitations, the obstacles he encounters in writing the book. In the first chapter—"The Palermo Section of Buenos Aires"—one reads: "The jumbled, incessant style of reality, with its punctuation of ironies, surprises, and intimations as strange as surprises, could only be recaptured by a novel, which would be out of place here." And how can he represent Palermo as it was before he knew it?

To recapture that almost static prehistory would be to foolishly weave a chronicle of infinitesimal processes. . . . The most direct means, according to cinematographic procedure, would be to propose a continuity of discontinuous images: a yoke of wine-bearing mules, the wild ones with their eyes blindfolded; a long, still expanse of water with willow leaves floating on the surface; a vertiginous will-o'-the-wisp wading through the flooding streams on stilts; the open countryside, with nothing to do there; the tracks of a hacienda's stubbornly trampled cattle path, the route to corrals in the north; a peasant (against the dawn sky) who dismounts and slits his jaded horse's wide throat; a wisp of smoke wafting through the air.

A relationship is established among these images. In "A Gossip on Romance" Stevenson had expounded his observations as a reader and sought support from them for his method as a writer. Borges, who agrees with those observations, sees them as applicable to the films of von Sternberg; and in his early *Evaristo Carriego*, where he doubts the very fiction whose elements he invokes, he attempts the magic of conjuring up a more abundant, unlimited reality by naming some notable moments that may postulate it. Film suggests to him the possibility of connecting those moments by means of a less discursive syntax than the verbal. Here a notion that might be termed *montage* appears, operating in texts made from words. That "cinematographic procedure," that "continuity of discontinuous images" will be the stated method in the stories of *Universal History of Infamy*. One of the chapters that divide—and integrate—"The Disinterested Killer Bill Harrigan" opens: "History (which like a certain director, proceeds by discontinuous images) now proposes the image of a. . . ."

The stories in *Universal History of Infamy* illustrate, point by point, Chesterton's observations in his study of Stevenson: "Those flat figures could only be seen from one side. They are aspects or attitudes of men rather than men" (*R. L. Stevenson*, London, 1928). The stories also illustrate what Chesterton noted about "our modern attraction to short stories" and the "short story today" in his study of Dickens: "We get a glimpse of grey streets of London, or red plains of India, as in an opium vision; we see people, arresting people with fiery and appealing faces. But when the story is ended, the people are ended" (*Charles Dickens*, London, 1906). To the degree that they ignore what Chesterton in his book on Stevenson calls "huge hospitality for their own characters" and, like Stevenson, prefer a certain thinness in characterization, a simplification appropriate to marionette theater, the two-dimensionality of colored illustrations, Borges's early fictional essays stage a narrative mechanism more than any particular narrative itself. And they do so with the clear awareness that the mechanism is identical in written and cinematographic fiction. (A connection can be seen between this procedure and *Nabokov's Dozen*, in which the destinies of various Russian adventurers, exiled in Berlin during the 1920s and linked occasionally to movies as extras, are recapitulated in takes, sequences, lighting effects, and montage in order to establish a parodic intent.)

There was a moment, which might be situated between *Evaristo Carriego* and the writing of his first story, "Man on the Pink Corner," when Stevenson and von Sternberg equally aroused Borges's attention, a moment when it seemed possible to submit Palermo's turn-of-the-century toughs as well as the neighborhood itself to a verbal treatment, the equivalent of von Sternberg's treatment of Chicago and its gangsters in *Underworld*. Impatient with the restraints that the novel seemed to impose on the exercise of fiction, Borges attempted fiction by cultivating a lucid magic. It matters little whether he was guided by the possibilities revealed to him in narratives by his favorite writers or if their writings permitted him to observe these possibilities in films.

5

Continuity and *discontinuity*: cinematographic language provided the point of departure for Borges's play with these concepts in his first attempts at fiction.

All narrative traditionally works by successive effects of continuity, with suspense deriving from an apparently defective continuity later restored by a postponed connection. Poetry, on the other hand, traditionally orders its emphases spatially, ignoring all requirements for connective relation other than the formal. Enumeration is one such relation, and Borges had cultivated it in his early fiction, obviously pleased with organizing his prose in a form unprecedented by the nineteenth-century novel. Every rhetorical work in the enumerative form invokes the supposed "endless variety of creation" by alluding to that creation with incongruous signs—a procedure whose illustrious, theological, and pantheistic genealogy cannot be reduced to Spitzer's "chaotic enumeration," which is linked to one notion of modernity. Nevertheless, a single characteristic is invariable: enumeration is always the double operation of naming in order to indicate the unnamed, of making the spaces between signs as denotative as the markers measuring their extension. Enumeration proposes to express the inexpressible; and, although it relies on only one scheme—enumeration—it is, like storytelling itself, syntactic by nature.

In enumeration, the discontinuity of the actual text seems to be endowed with the prestige of representing an absent, still greater text. Similarly, in *Discusión* and *Other Inquisitions*, Borges suggests that, far from denying the figure of Whitman, all the information about the poet's persona scattered throughout Whitman's work confirms his mythic stature. A comparable mechanism controls the lists of irreconcilable or merely dissimilar unities that dizzyingly sketch the infinite in such stories as "The Aleph," "The Zahir," "The God's Script," and even in the comparatively brief list of incarnations in "The Immortal."

By 1935, Borges's enumerations in *Universal History of Infamy* reveal how they function as concealed illusionism: they display properties of narrative usually disguised in the very act of being employed. The most famous example is the list of effects brought about by the fickle piety of Fray Bartolomé de las Casas in "The Terrible Redeemer Lazarus Morell." The terms in these enumerations—or the arguments united in a discourse—appear separated by what really connects them, as if by an electrical current: incongruity, paradox, simple otherness. At the same time, the enumerative combination as a whole registers the ironic richness of these minor clashes. Outside the circuit of conflict and ellipsis, these separate elements would lapse into the inertia of a historic or fictitious report uncharged by narrative.

It is no accident that, beginning with its title, an early Borges essay joins "narrative art" and "magic." His first fictions perform a kind of illusion: that *post hoc, ergo propter hoc*, an error in logic whose systematic cultivation, for Barthes, is the narrative operation par excellence, "the language of Fate." (Valéry also considered that associating the novelistic or even the fantastic world with reality was of the same order as associating trompe l'oeil with the tangible objects among which the viewer moves.) And what is that language of Fate if not an idea of montage? Cinematographic or verbal montage, which, in the chaotic archive of mankind's acts, proposes or discovers a meaning by ordering those "culminating moments" and "major scenes" in which Stevenson saw the proof and effect of the highest fiction? Stevenson saw it as operating on different levels of fiction and nonfiction, of history and fantasy. Its name, quite simply, is narrative.

---

[2] A novel by the Argentine writer Enrique Larreta (1875-1961). Published in 1908, the book reflects the influence of both literary realism and naturalism, especially in its extravagant devotion to historical detail. Cozarinsky says that Borges chose his example "magnaminously" since Borges did not ordinarily value Larreta's work.

BORGES ON FILM

My friends tell me that Pascal's thoughts stimulate their thinking. Surely there is nothing in the universe that does not serve to stimulate thought . . .

"Pascal," *Other Inquisitions*

FILMS

I am writing my opinion of some recent films.

The best, considerably surpassing the others: *Der Mörder Dimitri Karamasoff* (Filmreich). Its director, Ozep, appears to have had no difficulty in skirting the much praised and voguish flaws of the German film industry—lugubrious symbolism, tautology or meaningless repetition of equivalent images, obscenity, a propensity for teratology, and satanism—while at the same time avoiding falling into the still less resplendent errors of the Soviet school: total omission of characters, mere photographic anthologies, awkward charms of the Committee. (I will not even mention the French: thus far their one and only desire has been *not* to resemble the Americans—a risk, I assure them, they do not run.)

I am not familiar with the spacious novel from which this film was quarried—a *felix culpa* that allowed me to enjoy it without being continually tempted to superimpose the present movie on the remembered book in order to see if they coincided. So, with immaculate disregard for its irreverent desecrations and its spotless fidelities—both unimportant—I declare the present film extremely powerful. Its reality, although purely hallucinatory, with neither subordination nor cohesion, is no less torrential than the reality of Josef von Sternberg's *The Docks of New York*. The presentation of genuine, frank-hearted joy after a murder is one of its high points. The photographic sequences—approaching dawn, monumental billiard balls awaiting collision, Smerdiakov's clerical hand extracting the money—are excellent, both in conception and execution.

I pass on to another film. All our critics have unconditionally applauded Charlie Chaplin's latest, mysteriously entitled *City Lights;* but the truth behind this published acclaim has more to do with our faultless telegraphic and postal systems than with any presumptuous individual act of judgment. Would anyone dare overlook the fact that Charlie Chaplin is one of the established gods in the mythology of our time? A colleague of the motionless nightmares of de Chirico, the ardent machine guns of Scarface Al, the finite yet unlimited universe of Greta Garbo's summital shoulders, the glassed-in eyes of Ghandi? Could anyone not know beforehand that Chaplin's most recent *comédie larmoyante* was astonishing? In reality—in what I believe is reality—this much-seen film from the splendid creator and hero of *The Gold Rush* is nothing more than a weak collection of minor mishaps imposed on a sentimental story. Some of these episodes are new; one is not: the garbage collector's professional joy upon seeing the providential (and then deceiving) elephant, who is supposed to furnish him with a supply of raison d'être, is a facsimile reprint of the incident of the Trojan garbage collector and the fake Greek horse in that neglected film *The Private Life of Helen of Troy*.

More general objections can also be leveled against *City Lights*. Its lack of reality is comparable only to its—equally exasperating—lack of unreality. There are true-to-life pictures—*For the Defense, Street of Chance, The Crowd*, even *The Broadway Melody*—and there are willfully unrealistic pictures, such as the extremely individualistic ones of Frank Borzage, Harry Langdon, Buster Keaton, and Eisenstein. Chaplin's early escapades belong to the second type, undeniably based as they are on depthless photography and a ghostly speeding up of the action, as well as on the actors' fake moustaches, ridiculous artificial beards, fright wigs, and ominous overcoats. *City Lights* does not achieve such unreality, and it remains unconvincing. Except for the luminous blind girl—extraordinary in her beauty—and except for Charlie himself—always so disguised and wraith-like—all the film's characters are recklessly normal. Its ramshackle plot relies on the disjointed techniques of continuity from twenty years ago. Archaism and anachronism are also literary modes, I know; but their deliberate handling is different from their unfortunate perpetration. I relinquish my hope—too often fulfilled—of not being right.

One notices weariness, too, in von Sternberg's *Morocco*, even if to a less overwhelming and suicidal degree. Here, the terse photography, exquisite organization, and oblique yet suitable methods of *Underworld* have been replaced by mere hordes of extras and broad brushstrokes of local color. To indicate Morocco, von Sternberg has thought up nothing less vulgar than an over-elaborated forgery of a Moorish city in the Hollywood suburbs, with a superabundance of burnooses and fountains and tall guttural muezzins who precede the dawn and the camels in sunlight. On the other hand, the film's overall plot is good, and its resolution out in the open, in the desert, back at the starting point once more, corresponds to our first *Martín Fierro* or the novel *Sanin* by the Russian Artsybashev. One may watch *Morocco* with pleasure, but not with the intellectual satisfaction one gets from the first viewing (and even the second) of earlier works by von Sternberg. Not with the valid intellectual satisfaction produced by that heroic film *The Dragnet*.

SUR, No. 3, Winter 1931

Filmography

DER MÖRDER DIMITRI KARAMASOFF. Germany, 1931. *Director:* Fedor Ozep. *Screenplay:* Victor Trivas, Leonhard Frank, Fedor Ozep. *Based on the novel by* Fedor Dostoievsky. *Photography:* Friedl Behn-Grund. *Cast:* Fritz Kortner, Anna Sten, Fritz Rasp, Bernard Minetti, Max Pohl, Hanna Waag. A Terra picture.

THE DOCKS OF NEW YORK. U.S.A., 1928. 80 minutes. *Director:* Josef von Sternberg. *Screenplay:* Jules Furthman. *Based on a story by* John Monk Saunders. *Photography:* Harold Rosson. *Cast:* George Bancroft, Betty Compson, Olga Baclanova, Clyde Cook. A Famous Players-Lasky-Paramount picture.

CITY LIGHTS. U.S.A., 1930. 87 minutes. *Director, producer, author:* Charles Chaplin. *Photography:* Rollie Totheroh, Gordon Pollock, Mark Marklatt. *Cast:* Virginia Cherril, Florence Lee, Harry Myers, Allan García, Hank Mann, Charlie Chaplin. *Released by* United Artists.

THE GOLD RUSH. U.S.A., 1925. 72 minutes. *Director, producer, author:* Charles Chaplin. *Associate directors:* Charles Reisner, H. Abbadie d'Arrast. *Photography:* Rollie Totheroh, Jack Wilson. *Cast:* Charlie Chaplin, Mack Swain, Tom Murray, Georgia Hale, Betty Morissey. *Released by* United Artists.

THE PRIVATE LIFE OF HELEN OF TROY. U.S.A., 1927. 85 minutes. *Director:* Alexander Korda. *Screenplay:* Carey Wilson. *Based on the novel by* John Erskine *and the stage play by* Robert E. Sherwood. *Photography:* Lee Garmes *and* Sidney Hicock. *Cast:* Maria Corda, Lewis Stone, Ricardo Cortez, Alice White, George Fawcett. A First National picture.

FOR THE DEFENSE. U.S.A., 1930. 63 minutes. *Director:* John Cromwell. *Screenplay:* Oliver H. P. Garret. *Based on a story by* Charles Furthman. *Photography:* Charles Lang. *Cast:* William Powell, Kay Francis, Scott Kolk, William B. Davidson, John Elliott. A Paramount picture.

STREET OF CHANCE. U.S.A., 1930. 78 minutes. *Director:* John Cromwell. *Story:* Oliver H. P. Garret; *adapted by* Howard Estabrook; *dialogue:* Lenore J. Coffee. *Photography:* Charles Lang. *Cast:* William Powell, Jean Arthur, Kay Francis, Regis Toomey. A Paramount picture.

THE CROWD. U.S.A., 1928. 95 minutes. *Director:* King Vidor. *Screenplay:* King Vidor, John V. A. Weaver, Harry Behn. *Based on a story by* King Vidor.

Photography: Henry Sharp. *Cast:* Eleanor Boardman, James Murray, Bert Roach, Estelle Clark. An MGM picture.

THE BROADWAY MELODY. U.S.A., 1929. 104 minutes. *Director:* Harry Beaumont. *Story:* Edmund Goulding; *screenplay:* Sarah Y. Mason; *dialogue:* Norman Houston, James Gleason. *Photography:* John Arnold. *Cast:* Charles King, Bessie Love, Anita Page, Jed Prouty, Kenneth Thomson, Edward Dillon, Mary Doran. An MGM picture.

MOROCCO. U.S.A., 1930. 90 minutes. *Director:* Josef von Sternberg. *Screenplay:* Jules Furthman. *Based on the play "Amy Jolly" by* Benno Vigny. *Photography:* Lee Garmes. *Cast:* Gary Cooper, Marlene Dietrich, Adolphe Menjou. A Paramount picture.

UNDERWORLD. U.S.A., 1927. 83 minutes. *Director:* Josef von Sternberg. *Screenplay:* Robert N. Lee. *Based on a story by* Ben Hecht; *adapted by* Charles Furthman. *Photography:* Bert Glennon. *Cast:* Clive Brook, Evelyn Brent, George Bancroft, Larry Semon, Fred Kohler. *Producer:* Hector Turnbull. A Famous Players-Lasky-Paramount picture.

THE DRAGNET. U.S.A., 1928. 87 minutes. *Director:* Josef von Sternberg. *Screenplay:* Jules *and* Charles Furthman. *Based on the story "Nightstick" by* Oliver H. P. Garret. *Photography:* Harold Rosson. *Cast:* George Bancroft, Evelyn Brent, William Powell, Fred Kohler, Francis McDonald, Leslie Fenton. A Famous Players-Lasky-Paramount picture.

STREET SCENE

The Russians discovered that the oblique shot (and, consequently, the distorted shot) of a bottle, a bull's neck, or a column had greater esthetic value than Hollywood's thousand and one extras, quickly gotten up as Assyrians and then shuffled into total confusion by Cecil B. DeMille. They also discovered that the conventions of the Midwest—the merits of accusation and spying, of everlasting wedded bliss, the untarnished purity of prostitutes, the finishing uppercut dealt by a sober young man—could be exchanged for other, no less admirable conventions. (Thus, in one of the noblest Soviet films, a battleship bombards the overloaded port of Odessa at close range, with no casualties except for some marble lions. This marksmanship is harmless because it comes from a virtuous, maximalist battleship.)

Such discoveries were proposed to a world satiated to the point of disgust with Hollywood productions. The world respected these discoveries and extended its gratitude to the point of pretending that Soviet cinema had wiped out American cinema forever. (Those were the years when Alexander Blok announced, in the characteristic tones of Walt Whitman, that Russians were Scythians.) The world forgot, or tried to forget, that the greatest virtue of Russian films was their interruption of a steady diet from California. The world forgot that it was impossible to contrast some good, even excellent acts of violence (*Ivan the Terrible, Battleship Potemkin*, perhaps *October*) with a vast and complex literature, brought to happy fulfillment in all the genres, from the incomparably comic (Charlie Chaplin, Buster Keaton, and Harry Langdon) to the purely, inventively fantastic: the mythology of Krazy Kat and Bimbo. Alarm over the Russians grew. Hollywood reformed or enriched some of its photographic habits, and did not bother itself greatly.

King Vidor did. I am speaking of the uneven director of works as memorable as *Hallelujah* and as unnecessary and trivial as *Billy the Kid,* that shameful chronicling of the twenty murders (not counting Mexicans) committed by the famous fighter of Arizona, a film made with no other distinction than the accumulation of panoramic takes and the methodical elimination of close-ups in order to suggest the desert. His most recent work, *Street Scene,* adapted from the comedy of the same name by the ex-expressionist Elmer Rice, is inspired by the simple, negative desire not to look "standard." It has an unsatisfactory minimum of plot. It has a hero who is virtuous but under the influence of a thug. It has a romantic couple, but any civil or religious union is forbidden to them. It has a glorious, excessive Italian—larger than life—who evidently must take responsibility for all the comedy in the piece, a man whose unlimited unreality also rubs off on his normal colleagues. It has characters who seem true-to-life, and it has others in masquerade. Basically, it is not a realistic work; it is the repression or frustration of a romantic work.

Two great scenes elevate the film: the one of a dawn where the splendid course of the night is epitomized in music; the other of a murder indirectly presented to us in the tumult and tempest of faces.

Excellent actors and photography.

SUR, No. 5, Summer 1932

Filmography

STREET SCENE. U.S.A., 1931. 80 minutes. *Director:* King Vidor. *Screenplay:* Elmer Rice, *based on his original stage play. Photography:* George Barnes. *Cast:* Sylvia Sidney, William Collier, Jr., Estelle Taylor, Beulah Bondi, Max Montor. A Samuel Goldwyn Production *distributed by* United Artists.

CZAR IVAN THE TERRIBLE. U.S.S.R., 1926. 78 minutes. *Director:* Yuri Tarich. *Screenplay:* Konstantin Schildkret, Victor Shklovsky, Yuri Tarich. *Photography:* Mikhail Vladinirsky. Cast: Leonidov, I. Klyukvin, Nikolai Prozorovsky, Korsh, S. Askarova. A Sovkino picture.

BATTLESHIP POTEMKIN. U.S.S.R., 1925. *Director:* Sergei Eisenstein. *Screenplay:* Sergei Eisenstein, Nina Agadzhanova-Shutko. *Assistant Director:* Gregori Alexandrov. *Photography:* Eduard Tissé. *Cast:* A. Antonov, G. Alexandrov, V. Barsky, A. Levshin, M. Gomarov. A Goskino picture.

OCTOBER. U.S.S.R., 1927. 100 minutes. *Director:* Sergei Eisenstein. *Screenplay:* Sergei Eisenstein, Gregori Alexandrov. *Assistant Director:* Gregori Alexandrov. *Photography:* Eduard Tissé. *Cast:* Nikandrov, N. Popov, B. Livanov. A Sovkino picture.

HALLELUJAH. U.S.A., 1929. 108 minutes. *Director:* King Vidor. *Screenplay:* Wanda Tuchock; *dialogue:* Ransom Rideout. *Based on a story by* King Vidor *and a screen treatment by* Richard Schayer. *Photography:* Gordon Avil. *Cast:* Daniel L. Haynes, Nina Mae McKinney, William E. Fountaine, Harry Gray. An MGM picture.

BILLY THE KID. U.S.A., 1930. 98 minutes. *Director:* King Vidor. *Screenplay:* Wanda Tuchock; *dialogue:* Laurence Stallings; *additional dialogue:* Charles McArthur. *Based on "Saga of Billy the Kid" by* Walter Noble Burns. *Photography:* Gordon Avil. *Cast:* John Mack Brown, Wallace Beery, Kay Johnson, Wyndham Standing, Karl Dane. An MGM picture.

THE INFORMER

I am not familiar with the well-known novel from which this film was adapted: a *felix culpa* that has allowed me to watch it without the continual temptation to superimpose the present viewing on the recalled reading in order to test for coincidences. I have watched, and I consider it one of the best films offered us this past year. I consider it too memorable not to provoke a discussion and not to deserve a reproach. Several reproaches, really, since it has run the beautiful risk of being entirely satisfactory and, for two or three reasons, has not been.

The first is the excessive motivation for the hero's actions. I recognize that verisimilitude is the goal, but film directors—and novelists—are in the habit of forgetting that many justifications—and many circumstantial details—are counterproductive. Reality is not vague, but our general perception of reality is, and here lies the danger in over-justifying actions or inventing numerous details. In this particular case (that of the man suddenly turned Judas, the man who denounces his friend to the police, who hunt him down with their deadly machine guns), the erotic motive invoked seems, in some ways, to diminish the treachery of the deed and its heinous miracle. From an artistic point of view, infamy committed for amusement, for the mere brutality of infamy, would have been more impressive. I also think it would have been more believable. (Marcel L'Herbier's *Le Bonheur* is an excellent film invalidated by its excessive psychologizing of motives.) Obviously, the plurality of motives in itself does not seem bad to me. I admire the scene where the informer squanders his thirty pieces of silver because of his triple need to confuse, to bribe his threatening friends (who are perhaps his judges and will be his executioners at the end), and to rid himself of those banknotes that dishonor him.

Other weaknesses of *The Informer* are its beginning and end. The opening episodes do not ring true. In part, this is due to the street that is shown us—altogether too typical, too *European* (in the California sense of the word). Undeniably, a street in Dublin is not absolutely identical to a street in San Francisco, but it looks more like that street—since both are real streets—than like an obvious sham, jam-packed and weighed down with local color. More than universal similarities, local differences seem to have made a great impression on Hollywood: there is no American director, faced with the hypothetical problem of showing a railroad crossing in Spain or an uncultivated field in Austro-Hungary, who does not solve the problem by representing the site with a specially built set, whose only merit has to be the ostentation of its cost. As for the ending, I fault it for another reason. That the audience is moved by the horrifying fate of the informer seems appropriate; that the director of the film is moved and grants him a sentimental death accompanied by Catholic stained-glass windows and choir music seems less admirable.

In this film, the merits are less subtle than the faults and require no emphasizing. Nevertheless, I want to stress one very powerful touch: the dangling man's fingernails grating on the cornice at the very end and the disappearance of his hand as he is machine-gunned and falls to the ground.

Of the three tragic unities, two have been observed: the unities of action and time. The neglect of the third—unity of place—can be no cause for complaint. By its very nature, film seems to reject this third norm, requiring, instead, continuous displacements. (The dangers of dogmatism: the admirable memory of *Payment Deferred* cautions me against the mistake of generalizing. In that film, the fact that everything takes place in one house, almost in a single room, is a fundamental tragic virtue.)

SUR, No. 11, August 1935

Filmography

THE INFORMER. U.S.A., 1935. 91 minutes. *Director:* John Ford. *Screenplay:* Dudley Nichols. *Based on the novel by* Liam O'Flaherty. *Photography:* Joseph A. August. *Cast:* Victor McLaglen, Heather Angel, Preston Foster, Margot Grahame, Wallace Ford. Associate Producer: Cliff Reid. An RKO-Radio picture.

LE BONHEUR. France, 1934. 90 minutes. *Director:* Marcel L'Herbier. *Based on the play by* Henry Bernstein. *Additional dialogue:* Marcel L'Herbier. *Photography:* Harry Stradling. *Artistic collaborator:* Eve Francis. *Cast:* Charles Boyer, Gaby Morlay, Michel Simon, Jacques Catelain, Paulette Dubost. A Pathé-Natan picture.

PAYMENT DEFERRED. U.S.A., 1932. 8 reels. *Director:* Lothar Mendes. *Screenplay:* Ernest Vajda, Claudine West. *Based on the play by* Jeffrey F. Dell.

Photography: Merritt Gerstad. *Cast:* Charles Laughton, Neil Hamilton, Maureen O'Sullivan, Dorothy Peterson, Veree Teasdale, Ray Milland. An MGM picture.

TWO FILMS

One is called *Crime and Punishment,* by Dostoievsky/von Sternberg. That the first of these collaborators—the dead Russian—has not actually collaborated will astonish no one, given the practices of Hollywood; that the traces left by the second—the dream-filled Viennese—are equally unnoticeable borders on the monstrous. I can understand how the "psychological" novel might not interest a man, or might not interest him any longer. I could imagine that von Sternberg, a devotee of the inexorable Muse of Bric-à-Brac, might subordinate all the mental (or at least feverish) complexities of Rodion Romanovich's crime to the presentation of a pawnbroker's house crammed with intolerable objects or to a commissary identical to Hollywood's notion of a Cossack barracks. Indoctrinated by the populous memory of *The Scarlet Empress,* I was expecting a vast flood of artificial beards, mitres, samovars, masks, churlish faces, wrought-iron gates, vineyards, chess pieces, balalaikas, prominent cheekbones, and horses. In short, I was expecting the usual von Sternberg nightmare. I was waiting for the suffocation and the madness. In vain! For this film, von Sternberg has renounced his customary *marottes,* something that may be a very good omen. Unfortunately, he has not replaced them with anything. With no transition, with no break, he has merely passed from the state of hallucination *(The Scarlet Empress, The Devil Is a Woman)* to the condition of foolishness. Formerly, he seemed mad, which at least is something; now, merely simple-minded. Nevertheless, there is no cause for despair: it is possible that *Crime and Punishment,* a totally empty work, signifies an act of contrition and penitence, a necessary purification. It is possible that *Crime and Punishment* may link the dizzying sound and fury of *The Scarlet Empress* with a forthcoming film that will reject not only the peculiar charms of chaos but will also resemble—once again—intelligence. (In writing "once again" I am thinking of Josef von Sternberg's early films.)

From an extraordinarily intense novel, von Sternberg has extracted an empty film; from an absolutely dull adventure story—*The Thirty-nine Steps* by John Buchan—Hitchcock has drawn a good film. He has invented episodes. He has inserted wittiness and mischievousness where the original contained only heroism. He has introduced successful and completely unsentimental erotic relief. He has introduced a thoroughly delightful character—Mr. Memory—a man infinitely removed from the other two faculties of the soul, a man who reveals a grave secret simply because someone asks it of him and because to answer, at that moment, is his role.

SUR, No. 19, April 1936

Filmography

CRIME AND PUNISHMENT. U.S.A., 1935. *Director:* Josef von Sternberg. *Screenplay:* S. K. Lauren *and* Joseph Anthony. *Based on the novel by* Fedor Dostoievsky. *Photography:* Lucien Ballard. *Cast:* Peter Lorre, Edward Arnold, Marian Marsh, Tala Birell, Elizabeth Risdon, Robert Allen. *Producer:* B. P. Schulberg. A Columbia picture.

THE SCARLET EMPRESS. U.S.A., 1934. 13 reels. *Director:* Josef von Sternberg. *Screenplay:* Manuel Komroff, *based on Catherine the Great's diary. Photography:* Bert Glennon. *Cast:* Marlene Dietrich, John Lodge, Sam Jaffe, Louise Dresser, Maria Sieber, C. Aubrey Smith. A Paramount picture.

THE DEVIL IS A WOMAN. U.S.A., 1935. 85 minutes. *Director:* Josef von Sternberg. *Screenplay:* John Dos Passos. *Based on* Pierre Louys's *novel "La femme et le pantin." Photography:* Josef von Sternberg; *assistant photographer:* Lucien Ballard. *Cast:* Marlene Dietrich, Lionel Atwill, César Romero, Edward Everett Horton, Alison Skipworth. A Paramount picture.

THE THIRTY-NINE STEPS. England, 1935. 81 minutes. *Director:* Alfred Hitchcock. *Screenplay:* Charles Bennett and Alma Reville. *Based on the novel by* John Buchan. *Additional dialogue:* Ian Hay. *Photography:* Bernard Knowles. *Cast:* Madeleine Carroll, Robert Donat, Lucie Mannheim, Godfrey Tearle, Peggy Ashcroft. *Producer:* Michael Balcon; *associate producer:* Ivor Montagu. A Gaumont-British picture.

THE PETRIFIED FOREST

It is commonly observed that allegories are tolerable in direct proportion to their inconsistency and vagueness, which does not signify an apology for inconsistency and vagueness but, rather, a proof—a sign, at least—that the genre of allegory is a mistake. "The genre of allegory," I said, not the components or suggestions of allegory. (The best and most famous allegory, *The Pilgrim's Progress from This World to That Which Is to Come*, by the Puritan visionary John Bunyan, must be read as a novel, not as a prophecy; but if we eliminate all the symbolic justifications, the book will be absurd.)

The measure of allegory in *The Petrified Forest* is perhaps exemplary: light enough so as not to invalidate the drama's reality, substantial enough so as not to invalidate the drama's improbabilities. On the other hand, two or three weaknesses or pedantries in the dialogue continue to annoy me: a confused theological theory of neuroses, the summary (totally and minutely inaccurate) of a poem by T. S. Eliot, the forced allusions to Villon, Mark Twain, and Billy the Kid, contrived to make the audience feel erudite in recognizing those names.

Once the allegorical motive is dismissed or relegated to a secondary level, the plot of *The Petrified Forest*—the magical influence of approaching death on a random group of men and women—seems admirable to me. In this film, death works like hypnosis or alcohol: it brings the recesses of the soul into the light of day. These characters are extraordinarily distinct: the smiling, anecdotal grandfather, who sees everything as a performance and greets the desolation and bullets as a happy return to the turbulent normalcy of his youth; the weary gunman Mantee, as resigned to killing (and making others kill) as the rest are to dying; the imposing and absolutely vain banker with his diplomat's air of a great man of our conservative party; the young Gabrielle, who is given to attributing her romantic turn of mind to her French blood and her qualities as good *ménagère* to her Yankee origins; the poet, who advises her to reverse the terms of that attribution, which is so American—and so mythical.

I do not recall any other movies by Archie Mayo. This film (along with *The Passing of the Third Floor Back*) is one of the most intense that I have seen.

SUR, No 24, September 1936

Filmography

THE PETRIFIED FOREST. U.S.A., 1936. 83 minutes. *Director:* Archie Mayo. *Screenplay:* Charles Kenyon *and* Delmer Daves. *Based on the stage play by* Robert E. Sherwood. *Photography:* Sol Polito. *Cast:* Leslie Howard, Bette Davis, Genevieve Tobin, Dick Foran, Humphrey Bogart. *Associate producer:* Henry Blanke. A Warner Bros. picture.

THE PASSING OF THE THIRD FLOOR BACK. England, 1935. 8 reels. *Director:* Berthold Viertel. *Screenplay:* Michael Hogan, Alma Reville. *Based on a stage play by* Jerome K. Jerome. *Photography:* Curt Courant. *Cast:* Conrad Veidt, Rene Ray, Anna Lee, Frank Cellier. A Gaumont-British picture.

WELLS THE VISIONARY

The author of *The Invisible Man, The First Men in the Moon, The Time Machine,* and *The Island of Dr. Moreau*—I have cited his best novels, which are certainly not his most recent—has published the detailed text of his recent film, *Things to Come,* in a book of 140 pages. Did he do this, perhaps, in order to disassociate himself somewhat from that film? In order not to be held responsible for the whole of it? The suspicion is not illegitimate. For the time being, an initial chapter of instructions justifies or tolerates this suspicion.[3] There it is written that the men of the future will not be rigged up as telephone poles nor will they appear to be escapees from an electrical operating room nor will they run from one place to another encased in luminous suits made of cellophane, in glass jars, or in aluminium boilers: "I want Oswald Cabal," Wells writes, "to look like a fine gentleman, not a gladiator in his panoply or a padded lunatic. . . . No jazz, no nightmare stuff. In this more orderly world, there will have to be more time, more dignity. Let everything be roomier, bigger, but never monstrous."[4] Unfortunately, the grandiose film that we have seen—"grandiose" in the worst sense of that bad word—has very little to do with these intentions. To be sure, there are not a lot of cellophane boilers, aluminum neckties, padded gladiators, or madmen shining in their panoply; but the overall effect (much more important than the details) is of "nightmare stuff." I am not referring to the first part, where the monstrosity is deliberate; I am referring to the last, whose orderliness should oppose the bloody jumble of the first and which not only does not but, instead, exceeds the first in hideousness. Wells starts out by showing us the terrors of the immediate future, visited with plagues and bombardments. This exposition is very effective. (I recall a clear sky darkened and stained by airplanes as obscene and pestilential as locusts.) Then—I will use the author's words—"the film broadens out to display the grandiose spectacle of a reconstructed world." That "broadening out" is rather unfortunate: the heaven of Alexander Korda and Wells, like that of so many other eschatologists and scenographers, is not very different from their hell, and it is even less charming.

37

Another comparison: the book's memorable lines do not correspond—cannot correspond—to the film's memorable moments. On page 19, Wells speaks "of a jumble of quick flashes that show the confused inadequate efficiency of our world."[5] As might have been foreseen, the contrast of the words "confusion" and "efficiency" (not to mention the judgment in the epithet "inadequate") has not been translated into images. On page 56, Wells speaks of the masked aviator Cabal, "standing out against the sky, a tall portent."[6] The sentence is beautiful; its photographic version is not. (Even if it had been, it could never have corresponded to the sentence, since the arts of rhetoric and cinema—oh, classic ghost of Ephraim Lessing!—are absolutely incomparable.) On the other hand, there are successful sequences that owe nothing at all to the indications of the text.

Tyrants offend Wells but laboratories please him, hence his forecast of scientists joining together in order to unite a world wrecked by tyrants. Reality has yet to resemble his prophecy: in 1936, the power of almost all tyrants derives from their control of technology. Wells reveres chauffeurs and aviators; the tyrannical occupation of Abyssinia was the work of aviators and chauffeurs—and the fear, perhaps slightly mythological, of Hitler's depraved laboratories.

I have found fault with the film's second half; I insist on praising the first, with its wholesome effect for those people who still imagine war as a romantic cavalcade or a chance for wonderful picnics and free tourism.

SUR, No. 26, November 1936

Notes

[3] Borges refers to "Introductory Remarks," including a "Memorandum" that was "Circulated during production to everyone concerned in designing and making the costumes, decoration, etc. for the concluding phase (A.D. 2055) of *Things to Come*, London, 1935, pp. 9-16. The book has 142, not 140 pages, and this sort of rounding off and condensing typifies Borges's treatment of the text for his purposes—a treatment documented in the subsequent notes.

[4] Wells's text for the passage just quoted, as translated from Borges's translation, begins on page 15: "For such a man as Cabal I want a white or silver costume of very pure material. I want him to look like a fine gentleman, not a padded lunatic or an armoured gladiator." The phrases after the ellipsis in Borges's quotation occur on the next page, and read in the original: "But remember, fine clothes,

please; not nightmare stuff, not jazz." What follows in Borges's purported quotation, however, does not follow in Wells. In fact, what follows has already been paraphrased in the preceding sentences. First, a section from page 14: "People in the future will not be rigged up like telephone poles or as if they had just escaped from some sort of electrical operating room. They will not wear costumes of cellophane illuminated by neon lights or anything extravagant of that sort." Then the passage that Borges condenses and appends to his "quotation" that occurred still earlier on page 13: "Human affairs in that more organized world will not be hurried, they will not be crowded, there will be more leisure, more dignity. The rush and jumble and strain of contemporary life due to the uncontrolled effects of mechanism, are not to be raised to the nth power. On the contrary, they are to be eliminated. Things, structures, in general, will be great, yes, but they will not be monstrous."

[5] Borges adjusts Wells's syntax to his own and omits the phrase "multitudinousness, the hurry and" that follows the word "evoke" on page 19: "A rapid succession of flashes evokes the multitudinousness, the hurry and confused inadequate efficiency of our world."

[6] Again Borges adjusts the syntax to merge Wells's prose with his own. The original reads: "He stands out against the sky, a tall portent." In light of Borges's imagery in other books, it is interesting to note that the "masked aviator" is wearing a *gas* mask, a qualification that Borges suppresses. Wells's description is interesting in its own right: "He is dressed in shiny black and he wears a sort of circular shield over head and body that makes him over seven feet high. It is like a round helmet enclosing body as well as head. It is a 1970 gas mask. The vizor in front swings *down,* so that his head and shoulders seen from in front are suggestive of a Buddha against a circular halo. The black mask behind his head and shoulders is ribbed like a scallop shell. He stands out against the sky, a tall portent." *Things to Come,* p. 56.

Filmography

THINGS TO COME. England, 1936. 10 reels. *Director:* William Cameron Menzies. *Screenplay:* H. G. Wells, *based on his novel "The Shape of Things to Come." Photography:* Georges Perinal. *Cast:* Sir Cedric Hardwicke, Raymond Massey, Ralph Richardson, Sophie Steward, Ann Todd. *Producer:* Alexander Korda. A London Film Production picture.

FILM AND THEATRE

Allardyce Nicoll, who in the halls of wisdom of Yale University teaches a course on the history of drama, recently published a ponderous, large octavo volume about the "similarities and differences" between the secular theater and film. To lament the abysmal ignorance of this tome, whose bibliography lists 914 books and articles as well as upward of 200 periodicals, from *The Photodramatist* (Los Angeles) to *Das Publikum* (Charlottenburg), seems merely insolent. That ignorance, however, is not only incredible or improbable; it is also real. Professor Allardyce Nicholl, a man well versed in libraries, erudite in card catalogues, and sovereign in files, is almost illiterate in box-offices. He has rarely gone to the movies. To be more exact, he has been going to the movies only in the last few years. About the silent era, about the period before 1929, he knows next to nothing. About the present period, extremely little. Thus we can understand—but neither pardon nor defend—the omission of the works and names of Josef von Sternberg, Lubitsch, and King Vidor. As for his criteria, it is enough for me to transcribe this exemplary list of films that (according to him) justify the talking genre: *The House of Rothschild*, *The Private Life of Henry VIII*, *Queen Christina*, *David Copperfield*, *The Story of Louis Pasteur*, *Little Women*, *Catherine the Great*, *Man of Aran*, *The Informer*. Of these nine redeeming films, two—*The Informer* and *Catherine the Great*—are indisputably good; one—*Man of Aran*—is a mere anthology of images; another—*The Private Life of Henry VIII*—is not intolerable, while the remaining five justify, not to say demand, the burning down of the moviehouses where they play.

These two faults—appalling taste and inadequate information—should be enough, logically, to invalidate the book. Nevertheless, the facts of the case are more complex: Allardyce Nicoll's premises are debatable, but the conclusions he customarily derives from them are not. His application of these conclusions, on the other hand, can seem asinine. I shall cite an extreme example. On page 149, the author correctly establishes that

> *. . . in order to secure economy, visual images are preferable to words if these visual images are sufficient to convey the impression desired. Fundamental to the cinema is that which is pre-*

sented to the eye; this must ever take chief place. Words spoken occupy a secondary position; and printed words may only occasionally be called into service.[7]

Then he applies his law to a certain Laurel and Hardy film.* Here is the plot: L. and H. come to collect a legacy in a Scottish town, a mirror and paradigm of the most frigid virtues. A suitably Calvinistic and desiccated lawyer demands that they furnish proof of their identity. With an air of triumph, they take out some papers showing that they have been in jail, and then delightedly describe the perils and mishaps of their escape and voyage as stowaways on a cattle boat. With a gravity not unworthy of the lawyer, Professor Nicholl declares that their tale constitutes nothing more than a "retrospective narrative," that "retrospective narratives" are by nature dramatic, not cinematic, and, *as a consequence*, that the film should have begun in jail and shown the pair's escape, the chase after them, and their voyage across the Atlantic. Either I am very much mistaken or this objection is a veritable apotheosis of pedantry and formalism.

The mention of "retrospective narrative"—a literary device frequently found in the Homeric epics—leads us to a problem that the author discusses in the most interesting chapter of the book: the problem of cinematic time. Should esthetic time correspond to real time? The answers are multiple. Shakespeare—according to his own metaphor—put the accomplishments of many years into the turning of an hourglass; Joyce inverts the procedure and unfolds the single day of Leopold Bloom and Stephen Dedalus across the days and nights of the reader. More rewarding than the task of either shortening or lengthening a sequence is that of disarranging it, shuffling different times. In the realm of the novel, Faulkner and Joseph Conrad are the authors who have handled these inversions best; in film (which, as Allardyce Nicoll correctly observes, has singular means for producing such labyrinths and anachronisms) I recall only *The Power and the Glory* with Spencer Tracy. That film is the life story of a man that deliberately and movingly suspends chronological order. The first scene is his burial.

Another chapter studies the practice of interpolating images

---

*Bonnie Scotland, 1935. (E. C.)

with metaphoric value. Chaplin shows a crowd of workers entering a factory; then a second horde, this time of sheep, entering a pen. "Ah, the human flock!" the enraptured audience murmurs, quite satisfied with having immediately recognized this daring cinematic avatar of a literary commonplace. (What's more, everyone congratulates himself for his daringly radical reading of the metaphor.)

SUR, No. 26, November 1936

Notes

[7] *Film and Theatre*, New York, 1936. Characteristically, in translating the English text, which is quoted here in full, Borges compresses and edits the original—suppressing the entire last clause, for example, and adding "greater" before "economy" in the first.

Filmography

THE HOUSE OF ROTHSCHILD. U.S.A., 1934. 10 reels. *Director:* Alfred Werker. *Screenplay:* Nunnally Johnson. *Based on a stage play by* George Hembert Westley. *Photography (last sequence in Technicolor):* Peverell Marley. *Cast:* George Arliss, Loretta Young, Boris Karloff, Robert Young, C. Aubrey Smith. *Producer:* Darryl F. Zanuck. A 20th-Century Pictures production.

THE PRIVATE LIFE OF HENRY VIII. England, 1933. 97 minutes. *Director:* Alexander Korda. *Screenplay:* Lajos Biro *and* Arthur Wimperis. *Based on a story by* Arthur Wimperis. *Photography:* Georges Perinal. *Cast:* Charles Laughton, Robert Donat, Lady Tree, Binnie Barnes, Elsa Lanchester, Merle Oberon. A London Films Productions picture.

QUEEN CHRISTINA. U.S.A., 1933. 100 minutes. *Director:* Rouben Mamoulian. *Screenplay:* Salka Viertel *and* H. M. Harwood. *Based on a story by* Salka Viertel *and* Margaret P. Levine. *Dialogue:* S. N. Behrman. *Photography:* William Daniels. *Cast:* Greta Garbo, John Gilbert, Ian Keith, Lewis Stone, Elizabeth Young. *Producer:* Walter Wanger. An MGM picture.

DAVID COPPERFIELD. U.S.A., 1935. 133 minutes. *Director:* George Cukor. *Screenplay:* Howard Estabrook. *Based on the novel by* Charles Dickens, *adapted by* Hugh Walpole. *Photography:* Oliver T. Marsh. *Cast:* W. C. Fields, Lionel Barrymore, Maureen O'Sullivan, Madge Evans, Edna May Oliver, Lewis Stone, Freddie Bartholomew. *Producer:* David O. Selznick. An MGM picture.

THE STORY OF LOUIS PASTEUR. U.S.A., 1936. 85 minutes. *Director:* William Dieterle. *Screenplay:* Sheridan Libney, Pierre Collings. *Photography:* Tony Gaudio. *Cast:* Paul Muni, Josephine Hutchinson, Anita Louise, Donald Woods, Fritz Leiber. A Warner Bros. picture.

LITTLE WOMEN. U.S.A., 1933. 107 minutes. *Director:* George Cukor. *Screenplay:* Sarah Y. Mason *and* Victor Heerman. *Based on the novel by* Louisa May Alcott. *Photography:* Henry Gerrard. *Cast:* Katharine Hepburn, Joan Bennett, Frances Dee, Jean Parker, Spring Byington. *Producer:* David O. Selznick. An RKO Radio Pictures production.

CATHERINE THE GREAT. England, 1934. 10 reels. *Director:* Paul Czinner. *Screenplay:* Lajos Biro, Arthur Wimperis, Melchior Lengyel. *Based on a story by* Arthur Wimperis *and* Marjorie Deans. *Photography:* George Perinal. *Cast:* Elizabeth Bergner, Douglas Fairbanks, Jr., Flora Robson, Sir Gerald du Maurier. *Producer:* Alexander Korda. A London Film Productions picture.

MAN OF ARAN. England, 1934. 76 minutes. *Direction, screenplay, and photography:* Robert and Frances Flaherty. A Gainsborough Pictures Ltd. production for Gaumont British.

THE INFORMER. *See page 31.*

THE POWER AND THE GLORY. U.S.A., 1933. 76 minutes. *Director:* William K. Howard. *Screenplay:* Preston Sturges. *Photography:* James Wong Howe. *Cast:* Spencer Tracy, Collen Moore, Ralph Morgan, Helen Vinson. *Producer:* Jesse L. Lasky. A Fox picture.

TWO FILMS

I have seen two films on consecutive nights. The first—in both senses of that word—"is inspired by Joseph Conrad's novel *The Secret Agent*." The director himself declares so. Even without him, however, I must confess that I would have hit on the connection he points out, but never on that respiratory and divine verb *inspire*. Skillful photography, clumsy cinematography—those are the unimpassioned judgments that Hitchcock's latest film "inspires" in me. As for Joseph Conrad . . .

There can be no arguing that, aside from certain distortions, the story line of *Sabotage* (1936) coincides with the facts of the plot in *The Secret Agent* (1907); there also can be no arguing that the actions narrated by Conrad have a psychological value—have *only* a psychological value. Conrad offers for our understanding the destiny and character of Mr. Verloc, a lazy, fat, and sentimental man who comes to "crime" as a result of confusion and fear; Hitchcock prefers to translate him into an inscrutable Slavo-Germanic devil. An almost prophetic passage in *The Secret Agent* invalidates and refutes this translation:

But there was also about him an indescribable air which no mechanic could have acquired in the practice of his handicraft however dishonestly exercised: the air common to men who live on the vices, the follies, or the baser fears of mankind; the air of moral nihilism common to keepers of gambling halls and disorderly houses; to private detectives and inquiry agents; to drink sellers and, I should say, to the sellers of invigorating electric belts and to the inventors of patent medicines. But of that last I am not sure, not having carried my investigations so far into the depths. For all I know, the expression of these last may be perfectly diabolic. I shouldn't be surprised. What I want to affirm is that Mr. Verloc's expression was by no means diabolic.[8]

Hitchock has chosen to disregard this forewarning. I do not deplore his strange infidelity; I do deplore the petty task that he assigned himself. Conrad offers us complete understanding of a man who causes the death of a child; Hitchcock dedicates his art (and the slanting, sorrowful eyes of Sylvia Sidney) to making that death move us. The one man's undertaking was intellectual; the other's barely sentimental. That is not all: the film—oh complementary, insipid horror—adds an amorous episode whose characters, as chaste as they are enamored, are the martyred Mrs. Verloc and a dapper, good-looking detective, disguised as a greengrocer.

The other film is informatively titled *Los muchachos de antes no usaban gomina* (The Boys of Yesteryear Didn't Slick Down Their Hair). (Some informative titles are also beautiful: *The General Died at Dawn*.) This film—*Los muchachos de antes*, etc.—is unquestionably one of the best Argentine films I have seen, which is to say, one of the worst films in the world. The dialogue is absolutely unbelievable. The characters—doctors, toughs, and bullies of 1906—speak and live solely as a function of their difference from the people of 1937. They have no existence outside local and temporal color. There is a fistfight and another fight with knives. The actors neither know how to thrust and parry nor how to box, which slightly dims those spectacles.

The film's theme—"moral nihilism" in Buenos Aires, or the city's progressively going soft—is attractive, to be sure. The film's director wastes it. The hero, who ought to be emblematic of the old virtues—and the old treachery—is a citizen of Buenos Aires who has already been Italianized, a man cloyingly susceptible to the shameful seduction of apocryphal patriotism and sentimental tangos.

SUR, No. 31, April 1937

Notes

[8] Joseph Conrad, *The Secret Agent*, New York, 1907. Borges's translation is strict, except for his omission of the initial conjunction and the entire phrase between "there was" and "the air common to men. . . ."

Filmography

SABOTAGE. England, 1936. 76 minutes. *Director:* Alfred Hitchcock. *Screenplay:* Charles Bennett. *Based on the novel "The Secret Agent" by* Joseph Conrad, *adapted by* Alma Reville. *Dialogue:* Ian Hay, Helen Simpson, E. V. H. Emmett. *Photography:* Bernard Knowles. *Cast:* Sylvia Sidney, Oscar Homolka, Desmond Tester, John Loder. *Producers:* Michael Balcon, Ivor Montagu. A Gaumont British picture.

LOS MUCHACHOS DE ANTES NO USABAN GOMINA. Argentina, 1937. 90 minutes. *Direction and screenplay:* Manuel Romero. *Photography:* Francisco

Mugica. *Cast:* Florencio Parravicini, Mecha Ortiz, Santiago Arrieta, Irma Córdoba, Martín Zabalúa. A Lumiton picture.

THE GENERAL DIED AT DAWN. U.S.A., 1936. 98 minutes. *Director:* Lewis Milestone. *Screenplay:* Clifford Odets. *Based on the novel by* Charles G. Booth. *Photography:* Victor Milner. *Cast:* Gary Cooper, Madeleine Carroll, Akim Tamiroff, Dudley Digges, Porter Hall. *Producer:* William le Baron. An Adoph Zuckor production for Paramount.

LA FUGA

To enter a moviehouse on Lavalle Street in Buenos Aires and find myself (not without surprise) on the Gulf of Bengal or on Wabash Avenue seems preferable to entering that same moviehouse and finding myself (not without surprise) on Lavalle Street. I make this preliminary confession so that no one will attribute my defense of an Argentine film to murky feelings of patriotism. To idolatrize a ridiculous scarecrow because it is autochthonous, to fall asleep for the fatherland, to take pleasure in tedium because it is a national product—all seem absurd to me.

The primary virtue that may be distinguished in *La Fuga* (The Flight) is continuity. There are numerous films that never go beyond mere photographic anthologies—*The Passion of Joan of Arc* continues to be the mirror and archetype of this much praised error—and perhaps there is not a single European film that does not suffer from pointless images. In contrast, *La Fuga* flows limpidly, the way American films do. Buenos Aires, but Saslavsky spares us the Congreso, the Puerto de Riachuelo, the Obelisk; a ranch in the state of Entre Rios, but Saslavsky spares us the breaking in of horses, the branding of cattle, the two-horse 100 meter dash, the dueling guitars, and the all too predictably shrewd gauchos who boss around authentic Italians.[9]

The second virtue: the director has ignored the plot's tendency to be a tear-jerker. His villains practice murder the way someone practices a profession: they do not yearn for their native hut in elegiac tangos, and they are ruled by a serious German gentleman who delights in stuffed animals and lives in a functional house, thanks to the example of Gropius. It is true that one of the heroines gives up her life for her man, but it is just as true that she does not remain sexually faithful to him, as a North American director would have demanded. A detective helps her. This man (the surest and most admirable of touches) is much friendlier than the villains he chases.

The scene of the woman's death—the scene of her inaudible, dying voice—is the film's most intense. Another high point is the girl's astonishing joy on learning that two years—only two years—separate her from a joy she thought close at hand.

As for the defects ... I realize that with good logic we can reduce them to one: the slow-footed, painful comedy. *Mutatis mutandis*, the plot of *La Fuga* is that of Chaplin's famous film, *The Preacher*, badly rebaptized in Latin America as *El reverendo Caradura* (The Shameless Minister).* I do not disapprove of annexing this plot; I do disapprove of the ingenuous supposition that there are many grotesque possibilities left to explore in a story that has already been used by Chaplin. The ones *La Fuga* proposes to us—the young man who sits down on flypaper, the young man who holds a conversation with no pants on—are very awkward. Another, perhaps irreparable mistake: the insertion of farcical characters (in this case the principal of the little school) who contaminate the others with unreality. The others, and the story that lodges them.

SUR, No. 36, August 1937

---

*Borges is obviously thinking of *The Pilgrim*. (E.C.)

Notes

⁹Borges refers to local-color, postcard sites in the city of Buenos Aires: the Congreso square in the downtown area; the Italian district of the port known as La Boca; the obelisk commemorating the founding of the city and located in the center of the broad Avenida Nueve de Julio. Directly north of the province of Buenos Aires, Entre Rios is noted for its farming and ranching. Borges cites typical activities, taking advantage of the reference to scoff, again, at the conventionalized image of the gauchos.

Filmography

LA FUGA. Argentina, 1937. 92 minutes. *Director:* Luis Saslavsky. *Screenplay:* Alfredo G. Volpe. *Photography:* John Alton. *Cast:* Santiago Arrieta, Tita Merello, Francisco Petrone, Niní Gambier. A Pampa Film production.

LA PASSION DE JEANNE D'ARC. France, 1927. 110 minutes, cut to 86. *Director:* Carl Dreyer. *Screenplay:* Carl Dreyer, Joseph Delteil, *based on the original records of the trial*. *Photography:* Rudolph Maté. *Cast:* Maria Falconetti, Eugène Silvain, Maurice Schutz, Michel Simon, Antonin Artaud. A Société Générale de Films production.

THE PILGRIM. U.S.A., 1923. 4 reels. *Direction and screenplay:* Charles Chaplin. *Associate director:* Chuck Riesner. *Photography:* Rollie Totheroh. *Cast:* Charles Chaplin, Edna Purviance, Kitty Bradbury, Mack Swain, Loyal Underwood. A First National Films production.

GREEN PASTURES

Let us imagine a translation of the Bible to the time and space—conventional—of Gaucho literature. (It is impossible that someone has not already yielded to the temptation of trying this.) In such a reduction, the Devil is Mandinga, God is Daddy Dios, Abel is a rancher murdered by the farmer Cain, Pontius Pilate is the Commanding Officer, the Virgin Mary interrupts her hymn to the Holy Trinity in order to respond "Conceived without sin!" to the "Hail Mary, full of grace!" of a dusty, early-rising Angel, who has not even gotten off his wolf-gray horse. It is pointless to reveal other touches no less predictable and cumbersome: my readers can already get a foretaste of the special horror of this wild, Biblical hodge-podge. I want them to imagine it, and to detest it, so that I then may declare: That, precisely, is what *Green Pastures* is not.

To deny that identity is not to pretend that the bituminous Dead Sea—and Paradise—differ less from Louisiana or Georgia than from the Province of Buenos Aires. My thesis is different. I think that to appropriate the men of scripture or the men of Eduardo Gutiérrez[8] bothers us for the simple reason that it is an arbitrary procedure. (Which, let it be said between parenthesis, is the annoying original sin of our creole *Faust*—its joining of the 16th century to the 19th, of Saxony to Bragado, is totally haphazard.)[9] Not so Connelly's *Green Pastures*. The author states that "*The Green Pastures* is an attempt to present certain aspects of a living religion in the terms of its believers. The religion is that of thousands of Negroes in the deep South. With terrific spiritual hunger and the greatest humility these untutored black Christians—many of whom cannot even read the book that is the treasure house of their faith—have adapted the contents of the Bible to the consistencies of their everyday lives."[10] The numerous anachronisms (and anatropisms) that the adjustment gives rise to certainly do not exhaust the film's charms. We are amused when God saves the 10¢ cigar, which the Archangel has just offered him, "for later"; we are amused when rheumatic pains warn Noah of the approaching flood; we are amused when God, walking through the fields, asks some flowers how they are, and they answer him in unison, with a piping, child-like voice: "We O.K., Lawd."

People will tell me that the foregoing is ingenuous. I reply: yes, just as ingenuous as that "Lord God walking in the garden in the cool of the day" (Genesis 3:8). Do I dare add that I prefer the idea of a human God, an awkward God, a God capable of repenting, to the idea proposed by the theologians of a happily verbal monster, made up of three inextricable Persons and nineteen attributes? To the idea of a God about whom Wells said that he cannot act because he is all-powerful and eternal, cannot think because he is omniscient, cannot move because he is ubiquitous and is already everywhere.

SUR, No. 37, October 1937

Notes

[8] Eduardo Gutiérrez (1853-1890) was an Argentine author of numerous gauchesque novels in the serial or *folletín* manner.

[9] *Fausto,* a gauchesque poem published in 1870 by the Argentine poet Estanislao de Campo (1834-1880). In pointedly picturesque language, the poem gives the impression of one of the gauchos who has attended a performance of Gounod's *Faust*.

[10] Marc Connelly, *The Green Pastures*, New York, 1929, p. 55. Borges's translation conforms substantially to the opening paragraph of the "Author's Note," quoted here.

Filmography

GREEN PASTURES. U.S.A., 1936. 10 reels. *Directors:* Marc Connelly, William Keighley. *Screenplay based on the fable in dialogue by* Marc Connelly, *suggested by "Ol' Man Adam an' His Chillun," Southern tales by* Roark Bradford. *Photography:* Hal Mohr. *Cast:* Rex Ingram, Eddie Anderson, Oscar Polk. A Warner Bros. picture.

THE ROAD BACK

In the winter of 1872, among the jacaranda furniture of a hotel whose balconies faced the treeless Plaza de la Victoria, Don José Hernández—enemy of Sarmiento and of Mitre—wanted to expose the degradation that the disastrous military regime had produced in the natives of Buenos Aires and wrote the anti-war poem *The Gaucho Martín Fierro*. The hero—who doesn't know it?—was a deserter from the army; his companion a deserter from the police. We are familiar with the consequences. Around 1894, Unamuno discovered that Hernández's book "was the song of the Spanish fighter who, after having planted the cross in Granada, went to America to serve the progress of civilization and to open the road into the desert." In 1916, Lugones stated, "And for that reason—because it personifies the heroic life of the people with their language and their most genuine feelings, embodying it in a champion or, rather, in the most perfect emblem of justice and liberation—*Martín Fierro* is an epic poem."

I have recalled the instance of *Martín Fierro* because it is not unusual. Works denouncing the indignities or the horrors of war always run the risk of seeming to be a vindication of war. In fact, the more horrible the war, the greater its satanic prestige, the greater the virtue of those men who look it in the face. That obstinate Dr. Johnson, who once declared that "Patriotism is the last refuge of a scoundrel," also said, around 1778, "The profession of soldiers and sailors has the dignity of danger." What remains in our memory, right now, of the acclaimed pacifist film *All Quiet on the Western Front*? A fierce and enviable bayonet charge, exactly like the ones shown in any war movie.

The Road Back is undeniably inferior to *All Quiet on the Western Front*. Its climactic moment is also a battle. The peculiar pathos of the scene comes from its being absolutely clear to us that the soldiers' fears and agonies are futile: Germany had already surrendered. The other scenes, it seems to me, are entirely forgettable. The thesis (I think) is the unadaptability of soldiers to civilian life, the conflict between the ethic of the city and the ethic of the trench. Fear of rendering the protagonists disagreeable has dulled—or invalidated—the demonstration of this thesis. It is true that one of the veterans ends up a murderer, but his victim is such an execrable, such an oily, such a minutely Jewish *Schieber* that his destruction is a worthy act in any light. Another of the veteran fighters ends up in a marriage of convenience, another improvising speeches, another coveting (and stealing) other people's chickens.

On seeing *The Road Back* I felt that mere pacifism is not enough. War is an ancient passion that tempts men with ascetic and mortal charms. In order to abolish it, you have to confront it with another passion. Maybe that of the *good European*—Leibniz, Voltaire, Goethe, Arnold, Renan, Shaw, Russell, Unamuno, T. S. Eliot—who recognizes himself as the heir and the perpetuator of all countries. Unfortunately, Europe is teeming with mere Germans and mere Irishmen. Europeans are scarce.

SUR, No. 38, November 1937

Filmography

THE ROAD BACK. U.S.A., 1937. 12 reels. *Director:* James Whale. *Screenplay:* R. C. Sherriff, Charles Kenyon. *Based on the novel by* Erich Maria Remarque. *Photography:* John Mescall. *Cast:* John King, Richard Cromwell, "Slim" Summerville, Andy Devine, Louise Fazenda. *Associate Producer:* Edmund Grainger. A Universal picture.

ALL QUIET ON THE WESTERN FRONT. U.S.A., 1930. 140 minutes. *Director:* Lewis Milestone. *Screenplay:* Del Andrews, Maxwell Anderson, George Abbott, *with dialogue by* Anderson and Abbott. *Based on the novel by* Erich Maria Remarque. *Photography:* Arthur Edeson. *Cast:* Lewis Ayres, Louis Wolheim, John Wray, George "Slim" Summerville, Russell Gleason. Producer: Carl Laemmle, Jr. A Universial picture.

PRISIONEROS DE LA TIERRA

Two characters join their futile forces to make *Prisioneros de la tierra* (Prisoners of the Earth) intolerable, unwatchable. One: the huge and staggering Dr. Else, an unrecognized precursor of *ultraísmo* ("The red earth imprisons men . . ."; "I have been wrapped in a moist sudarium for twenty-five years. . . .")[13] who parades his face—an enormous lion's or king's, straight off a playing card—from one end of the film to the other and succeeds in being no less overwhelming than the frightful Emil Jannings. The other: a certain amateur encyclopedist who shakes his mutilated arm with joyful persistence and repeats over and over: "I am a happy man. What more do I need to be happy?" Or, "Don't you know that to love is to understand?"

In spite of these "conversationists," the film is good, even very good. It is superior—faint praise!—to many that our resigned republic has given birth to (and applauded). It is also superior to most of the films that California and Paris have sent us recently. One incredible and sure touch: there is not a single comic scene in the course of this exemplary film. To ignore Sandrini, to successfully elude Pepe Arias, and to avert Catita are three forms of happiness our directors have not entered upon before now.[14] Clearly, these negative merits are not the only ones.

There is a powerful plot, uncontaminated by either virginal North American tawdriness (in the first scene, the protagonist walks out of a brothel) or by that other neo-tawdriness, which in every French film gives us a fleeting, epigrammatic glimpse of a pair of lovers. There is a character—the vicious Koerner (with his core of unviolated loneliness, his Beethoven record, and his resigning himself to being cruel and hated), who certainly is more lifelike than the hero. I have been—which of my friends doesn't know it?—an insatiable and fervent patron of Milton Sills, of Kohler, and of Bancroft;[15] I do not recall, in such a bloody picture, a more powerful scene than the next-to-last in *Prisioneros de la tierra*, where the man is horsewhipped into a final river. That man is brave, that man is arrogant, that man is taller than the other . . . In similar scenes in other pictures, brutal people are appointed to perform brutal actions; in *Prisioneros de la tierra* the hero is appointed, and he is almost intolerably efficient. (If I am not mistaken, this wonderful assignment is the handiwork of Ulyses Petit de Murat; the two actors perform the scene very well.)

Another memorable moment occurs when, from his horse, one of the maté plantation owners kills the half-enslaved peon with a single, laconic bullet and does not even turn his head to see his victim fall; still another: the woman's passionate flight through the tremulous mountain night.

Photography, admirable.

SUR, No. 60, September 1939

Notes

[13] A literary movement that Borges introduced to Argentina on his return from Europe in 1921. It was characterized by an attempt to reduce poetry to paratactic images and metaphors. Borges later repudiated this phase of his literary career.

[14] Luis Sandrini started in the movies with the advent of sound and immediately became the most popular comic actor in Argentina; Niní Marshall, a comic actress in films of the '40s and '50s, gained fame on the radio with a series of sterotyped characters, including the semi-illiterate "Catita"; José Arias, who came to the movies from theater revues, acted in films from the '20s to the mid-'50s.

[15] Three leading men of Hollywood: Milton Sills (1882-1930) starred in many silent movies such as *The Claw* (1917) and *The Sea Wolf* (1930); Fred Kohler (1889-1938) specialized as a villain in Westerns such as *The Iron Horse* (1924); and George Bancroft played toughs and villains in movies like *The Docks of New York* (1928) and *Scandal Sheet* (1931). Both Kohler and Bancroft appeared in von Sternberg's *Underworld* (1927) and *The Dragnet* (1928).

Filmography

PRISIONEROS DE LA TIERRA. Argentina, 1939. 85 minutes. *Director:* Mario Soffici. *Screenplay:* Darío Quiroga, Ulyses Petit de Murat. *Based on stories by* Horacio Quiroga. Photography: Pablo Tabernero. *Cast:* Francisco Petrone, Angel Magaña, Roberto Fugazot, Homero Cárpena, Elisa Galvé. A Pampa Film production.

AN OVERWHELMING FILM

Citizen Kane (called *The Citizen* in Argentina) has at least two plots. The first, of an almost banal imbecility, tries to milk applause from the very unobservant. It may be formulated in this way: a vain millionaire accumulates statues, orchards, palaces, swimming pools, diamonds, cars, libraries, men and women. Like an earlier collector (whose observations are traditionally attributed to the Holy Ghost), he discovers that these miscellanies and plethoras are vanity of vanities, all is vanity. At the moment of his death, he yearns for a single thing in the universe: a fittingly humble sled that he played with as a child!

The second plot is far superior. It links Koheleth [16] to the memory of another nihilist: Franz Kafka. The theme (at once metaphysical and detective-fictional, at once psychological and allegorical) is the investigation of a man's secret soul by means of the works he has made, the words he has spoken, the many destinies he has destroyed. The procedure is the same as in Joseph Conrad's *Chance* (1914) and the beautiful film *The Power and the Glory*: a rhapsody of heterogeneous scenes, out of chronological order. Overwhelmingly, endlessly, Orson Welles shows fragments of the life of the man, Charles Foster Kane, and invites us to combine them and to reconstruct him. The film teems with forms of multiplicity, of incongruity: the first scenes record the treasures amassed by Kane; in one of the last, a poor woman, sumptuous and suffering, plays with an enormous jigsaw puzzle on the floor of a palace that is also a museum. At the end, we realize that the fragments are not governed by any secret unity: the detested Charles Foster Kane is a simulacrum, a chaos of appearances. (A possible corollary, foreseen by David Hume, Ernst Mach, and our own Macedonio Fernández: no man knows who he is, no man is anyone.) In one of Chesterton's stories—"The Head of Caesar," I think[17]—the hero observes that nothing is so frightening as a labyrinth with no center. This film is precisely that labyrinth.

We all know that a party, a palace, a great undertaking, a lunch for writers and journalists, an atmosphere of light-hearted and spontaneous camaraderie are essentially horrible. *Citizen Kane* is the first film that shows these things with some awareness of this truth.

In general, the film's execution is worthy of its vast subject. There are shots with admirable depth, shots whose farthest planes (as in the paintings by the Pre-Raphaelites) are no less precise and detailed than the closest.

Nevertheless, I venture to guess that *Citizen Kane* will endure as certain of Griffith's or Pudovkin's films have "endured"— films whose historical value no one denies, films no one especially wants to see again. *Citizen Kane* suffers from gigantism, from pedantry, from tediousness. It is not intelligent, it is a work of *genius*—in the most nocturnal and Germanic sense of that bad word.

SUR, No 83, August 1941

Notes

[16] Ecclesiastes, as in *A Gentle Cynic, Being a Translation of the books of Koheleth, Commonly Known as Ecclesiastes* by Morris Jastrow, Jr., Philadelphia, 1919.

[17] G. K. Chesterton, *The Father Brown Stories*, London, 1929, p. 235: "'What we all dread most,' said the priest in a low voice, 'is a maze with *no* centre. That is why atheism is only a nightmare.'"

Filmography

CITIZEN KANE. U.S.A., 1941. 119 minutes. *Director:* Orson Welles. *Screenplay:* Orson Welles, Herman J. Mankiewicz. *Photography:* Gregg Toland. *Cast:* Orson Welles, Joseph Cotten, Dorothy Comingore, Agnes Moorehead, Ruth Warrick, Ray Collins. *Producer:* Orson Welles. Produced by Mercury for RKO Pictures.

THE POWER AND THE GLORY. *See page 43.*

DR. JEKYLL AND MR. HYDE TRANSFORMED

For the third time, Hollywood has defamed Robert Louis Stevenson. In Argentina, this defamation is called *El hombre y la bestia* (The Man and the Beast): it has been perpetrated by Victor Fleming, who repeats with unfortunate fidelity the esthetic and moral errors of the version—of the perversion—by Mamoulian. I shall begin with the latter, the moral errors.

In the 1886 novel, Dr. Jekyll is morally double, in the way all men are double, while his hypostasis—Edward Hyde—is fiendish without respite and without alloy; in the 1941 film, Dr. Jekyll is a young pathologist who practices chastity while his hypostasis—Hyde—is a profligate with traces of the sadist and the acrobat. For the philosophers in Hollywood, Good is the courtship of the chaste and wealthy Miss Lana Turner; Evil (which similarly concerned David Hume and the heresiarchs of Alexandria), illegal cohabitation with Fröken Ingrid Bergman or Miriam Hopkins. Futile to note that Stevenson is completely innocent of this limitation or deformation of the problem. In the book's last chapter, he declares the vices of Jekyll: sensuality and hypocrisy; in one of the *Ethical Studies*—from the year 1888—he tries to list "all the displays of the truly diabolic" and proposes the following: "envy, malice, the mean lie, the mean silence, the calumnious truth, the backbiter, the petty tyrant, the peevish poisoner of family life."[18] (I would affirm that ethics do not include sexual matters so long as they are not contaminated by treason, greed, or vanity.)

The structure of the film is even more rudimentary than its theology. In the book, the identity of Jekyll and Hyde is a surprise: the author saves it for the end of the ninth chapter. The allegorical tale pretends to be a detective story; no reader guesses that Hyde and Jekyll are the same person. The very title of the book makes us postulate them as two. Nothing easier than to transfer this device to the screen. Let us imagine any detective mystery: two actors, well known to the public, figure in the plot (George Raft and Spencer Tracy, let's say); they may use analogous words, they may refer to events that presuppose a common past. When the mystery remains unsolved, one of them swallows the magic drug and changes into the other. (Of course the successful execution of this plan would allow for two or three phonetic adjustments: the changing of the protagonists' names.) More civilized than I, Victor Fleming avoids all surprise and mystery: in the early scenes of the film, Spencer Tracy fearlessly drinks the versatile potion and transforms himself into Spencer Tracy, with a different wig and Negroid features.

Going beyond Stevenson's dualist parable and getting closer to the *Parliament of the Birds*, which Farid al-din Attar composed in the 12th century of the Christian era,[19] we may imagine a pantheistic film, whose numerous characters finally resolve into One, who is everlasting.

SUR, No. 87, December 1941

Notes

[18] Borges's translation conforms to Stevenson's original, which is quoted here from "A Christmas Sermon," *Ethical Studies*, vol. 26, p. 71, *Collected Works*, 1924.

[19] Borges refers to this work several times in his writings, including the entry under "El Simurg" in *The Book of Imaginary Beings*, translated by Norman Thomas di Giovanni in collaboration with Borges, New York, 1969. The myth tells of a group of birds that set out to find the Simurg, the king of the birds. Finally, thirty of them reach their destination, only to realize that they are the Simurg and that the Simurg is each and all of them. Edward FitzGerald translated parts of the poem as *The Bird-parliament: A bird's eye view of Farid-Uddin Attar's Bird-parliament*.

Filmography

DR. JEKYLL AND MR. HYDE. U.S.A., 1941. 127 minutes. *Director:* Victor Fleming. *Screenplay:* John Lee Mahin. *Based on the novel by* Robert Louis Stevenson. *Photography:* Joseph Ruttenberg. *Cast:* Spencer Tracy, Ingrid Bergman, Lana Turner, Donald Crisp. *Producer:* Victor Fleming. An MGM picture.

TWO FILMS

They say that the doctrines of the transmigration of souls and of circular time or the Eternal Return were suggested by paramnesia, by a sudden, disturbing impression of having already lived the present moment. In Buenos Aires, at 6:30 and 10:45 p.m., there is not a single movie-goer, no matter how forgetful, who does not experience that impression.

For many years, Hollywood (like the Greek tragedians) has stuck, in effect, to ten or twelve plots: the aviator who, by means of a convenient catastrophe, dies in order to save the friend whom his wife loves; the deceitful typist who does not refuse the gifts of furs, apartments, tiaras, and cars but who slaps or kills the giver when he "goes too far"; the unspeakable and renowned reporter who seeks the friendship of a gangster with the sole motive of betraying him and making him die on the gallows . . .

The latest victim of this disconcerting asceticism is Miss Bette Davis. They have made her act out the following romance: a woman, weighed down by a pair of spectacles and a tyrannical mother, considers herself insipid and ugly; a psychiatrist (Claude Rains) persuades her to vacation among palm trees, to play tennis, to visit Brazil, to take off the spectacles, to change dressmakers. The five-part treatment works: the captain of the ship bringing her home repeats with obvious truthfulness that not one of the other women aboard has had Miss Davis's success. Prior to this endorsement, a niece, previously formidable in her sarcasm, now sobbingly begs forgiveness. Then the film's bold thesis spreads across the screens of the most remote moviehouses: *Disfigured, Miss Davis is less beautiful.*

The deformed comedy I have summarized is called *Now Voyager*. It was directed by a certain Irving Rapper, who, quite possibly, may not be a fool. Unfortunately, this is how they degrade the tragic heroine of *The Little Foxes*, *The Letter*, *Of Human Bondage*.

The film *Nightmare* is less ambitious and more tolerable. It begins as a detective film; it wastes no time in lapsing into an irresponsible adventure film. It suffers from all the defects of both genres; it has the sole virtue of not belonging to the *genre ennuy-*

eux. Its plot is one of those that has surprised every spectator hundreds of times: the duel of a fair girl and an average man with an all-powerful and malicious society, which before the war was China and now is the Gestapo or the international spies of the Third Reich. Two purposes goad the luckless directors of such films: the first is to show that Orientals (or Prussians) combine the perfection of evil with the perfections of intelligence and treachery; the second, to show that there is no man of good will who does not succeed in outwitting them. Inevitably, these incompatible propositions cancel each other. Various and impending dangers threaten the heroine and hero. These perils turn out to be imaginary and ineffectual since the spectators know very well that the film must last for an hour—a famous fact that guarantees the protagonists a longevity or immortality of sixty minutes. Another convention that invalidates pictures of this sort is the superhuman courage of the protagonists: they are told they are going to die, and they smile. The audience smiles too.

SUR, No. 103, April 1943

Filmography

NOW VOYAGER. U.S.A., 1942. 118 minutes. *Director:* Irving Rapper. *Screenplay:* Casey Robinson. *Based on the novel by* Olive Higgins Prouty. *Photography:* Sol Polito. *Cast:* Bette Davis, Paul Henreid, Claude Rains, Gladys Cooper, Bonita Granville, Ilka Chase, John Loder. *Producer:* Hal B. Wallis. A Warner Bros. picture.

THE LITTLE FOXES. U.S.A., 1941. 115 minutes. *Director:* William Wyler. *Screenplay:* Lillian Hellman, *based on her stage play with additional scenes and dialogue by* Arthur Kober, Dorothy Parker, Alan Campbell. *Photography:* Gregg Toland. *Cast:* Bette Davis, Herbert Marshall, Teresa Wright, Richard Carlson, Dan Duryea. *Producer:* Samuel Goldwyn. An RKO Radio Pictures film.

THE LETTER. U.S.A., 1940. 95 minutes. *Director:* William Wyler. *Screenplay:* Howard Koch. *Based on the stage play by* W. Somerset Maugham. *Photography:* Tony Gaudio. *Cast:* Bette Davis, Herbert Marshall, James Stephenson, Frieda Inescort, Gale Sondergaard. *Producer:* Hal B. Wallis; *associate producer:* Robert Lord. A Warner Bros. picture.

OF HUMAN BONDAGE. U.S.A., 1934. 83 minutes. *Director:* John Cromwell. *Screenplay:* Lester Cohen. *Based on the novel by* W. Somerset Maugham. *Photography:* Henry W. Gerrard. *Cast:* Leslie Howard, Bette Davis, Frances Dee, Kay Johnson, Reginald Denny, Alan Hale. *Producer:* Pandro S. Berman. An RKO Radio Pictures film.

NIGHTMARE. U.S.A., 1942. 8 reels. *Director:* Tim Whelan. *Screenplay:*

Dwight Taylor, *based on a story by* Phillip MacDonald. *Photography:* George Barnes. *Cast:* Diana Barrymore, Brian Donlevy, Gavin Muir, Henry Daniell, Hans Conreid. *Producer:* Dwight Taylor. A Universal Pictures film.

ON DUBBING

The possibilities for the art of combination are not infinite, but they are apt to be frightening. The Greeks engendered the chimera, a monster with the head of a lion, the head of a dragon, and the head of a goat; the theologians of the second century, the Trinity, in which the Father, the Son, and the Holy Ghost are inextricably linked; the Chinese zoologists, the *ti-yiang*, a bright red, supernatural bird equipped with six feet and six wings but with neither face nor eyes; the geometrists of the nineteenth century, the hypercube, a four-dimensional figure that encloses an infinite number of cubes and is bounded by eight cubes and twenty-four squares. Hollywood has just enriched this frivolous, teratological museum: by means of a perverse artifice they call dubbing, they offer monsters that combine the well-known features of Greta Garbo with the voice of Aldonza Lorenzo. How can we fail to proclaim our admiration for this distressing prodigy, for these ingenious audio-visual anomalies?

Those who defend dubbing will reason (perhaps) that the objections to it can be brought, similarly, against any other example of translation. This argument ignores, or avoids, the central fault: the arbitrary grafting of another voice and another language. The voice of Hepburn or Garbo is not accidental; it is, for the whole world, one of their defining attributes. Similarly, it is worth remembering that miming is different in English and Spanish.*

I have heard that they enjoy dubbing in the provinces. That is a simple argument from authority, and so long as they do not publish the syllogisms of the connoisseurs from Chilecito and Chivilcoy,[20] I, at least, shall not let myself be intimidated. I also hear that people who do not know English find dubbing delightful, or tolerable. My comprehension of English is less perfect than my incomprehension of Russian; nevertheless, I would never resign myself to seeing *Alexander Nevsky* again in any language other than the original, and I would see it eagerly, for the ninth or tenth time, if they showed it in the original version or one that I be-

---

*More than one spectator asks himself: Since there is usurpation of voices, why not of faces as well? When will the system be perfect? When will we see Juana González directly, in the role of Greta Garbo, in the role of Queen Christina of Sweden? (J.L.B.)

lieved to be the original. This last point is important: worse than dubbing, worse than the substitution that dubbing implies, is the widespread awareness of a substitution, of a deception.

There is no advocate of dubbing who does not wind up invoking predestination and determinism. They swear that this expedient is the result of an inevitable evolution and that soon we will have to choose between seeing dubbed films and not seeing films at all. Given the world-wide decadence of motion pictures—hardly reformed by any single exception such as *The Mask of Demetrios*—the second of these alternatives is not painful. Recent bad pictures—I am thinking of Moscow's *The Diary of a Nazi* and Hollywood's *The Story of Dr. Wassell*—prompt us to judge movies as a kind of negative paradise. "Sightseeing is the art of disappointment," Stevenson noted. The definition applies to films and, with sad frequency, to that continuous, unavoidable exercise called life.

SUR, No. 128, June 1945

Notes

[20]Two provincial towns, the former in central Rioja province, the latter in northern Buenos Aires province.

Filmography

ALEXANDER NEVSKI. U.S.S.R., 1938. 110 minutes. *Director:* Sergei Eisenstein. *Screenplay:* Sergei Eisenstein, Piotr Paylenko. *Photography:* Eduard Tissé. *Music:* Sergei Prokofiev. *Cast:* Nikolai Cherkasov, Nikolai Ojlopkov, Alexander Abrikosov, Dimitri Orlov, Vasili Novikov, Nikolai Arsky, Varvara Massalinitova. A Mosfilm picture.

THE MASK OF DIMITRIOS. U.S.A., 1944. 95 minutes. *Director:* Jean Negulesco. *Screenplay:* Frank Gruber. *Based on the novel "A Coffin for Dimitrios" by* Eric Ambler. *Photography:* Arthur Edeson. *Cast:* Zachary Scott, Peter Lorre, Sidney Greenstreet, Faye Emerson, Victor Francen. *Producer:* Henry Blanke. A Warner Bros. film.

VOEVOI KINOSBORNIK No. 9 *(Diary of a Nazi)*. U.S.S.R., 1942. Number 9 in a series of film sketches called *Moviereview of War* or *Fighting Film Albums*. *Supervisor:* Mark Donskoi. Episode *District 14: Director:* Igor Savchenco. *Story:* Salomon Lazurin. Episode: *The Blue Ravine: Director:* Vladimir Braun. *Story:* L. Smirnova, S. Gergel. Episode: *The Sign: Director:* Mark Donskoi. *Story:* N. Severov, I. Olesha. *Photography:* Y. Ekelchik, D. Demutsky, A. M. Mishurin. *Cast:* M. Bernes, I. Anazhevskaya; N. Komissarov, L. Kmit; V. Mironova, V.

Runge, N. Bubnov, H. Klering, S. Ditlovich, L. Kmit. Produced by the Kiev and Ashkhabad Studios.

THE STORY OF DR. WASSELL. U.S.A., 1944. *Director:* Cecil B. De Mille. *Screenplay:* Alan Le May, Charles Bennett. *From a story by* James Hilton *based on war records. Photography (Technicolor):* Victor Milner, William Snyder. *Cast:* Gary Cooper, Laraine Day, Signe Hasso, Dennis O'Keefe. *Producer:* Cecil B. De Mille. A Paramount film.

FIVE BRIEF ITEMS*

King Kong: A monkey fourteen meters high (some of his fans say fifteen) is obviously charming, but perhaps that is not enough. This monkey is not full of juice; he is a dried out and dusty contraption with angular, clumsy movements. His only virtue—his height—seems not to have greatly impressed the photographer, who persists in not shooting him from below but from above, a plainly mistaken angle that invalidates and annuls his tallness. It should be added that he is hunchbacked and bowlegged, features that also shorten him. To ensure that there is nothing extraordinary about him, they make him fight monsters far stranger than he and find him lodgings in fake caverns the size of a cathedral, where his hard-won stature is lost. A carnal or romantic love for Miss Fay Wray brings to perfection the ruin of this gorilla and of the film as well.

She Done Him Wrong: Two slight faults must be pardoned in this film: one is the incoherent ending, which seems like a last-minute change of mind; the other, the horrendous Spanish title, *Nacida para pecar* (Born to Sin), which drove away many viewers, perhaps even the best ones. With the exception of these minor errata, the film is interestingly satisfactory. Mae West, in her role as a splendid floozy, as a physical woman, notably surpasses Jean Harlow and—why not say it—Marlene. She sings some sorrowful blues that I want to hear again the third time I see the film. The setting—gaudy, vulgar New York at the turn of the century, with its neighborhood bosses, its dandies with tilted tophats and straight six-shooters, its busy prostitutes with cinched waists and delicate hairdos, its nasal Methodist hymns, its accusations, sudden rages and parties—is touching.

Kongo: Another title to scare you away and another excellent film. It is neither about wary, haughty hunters with troops of blacks and lions with obligations to the camera nor about botanical and zoological catalogues. It seems unbelievable, but this film is not afflicted by a single Spanish commentator among those

---

*See "A Footnote for the English-language Edition," p. 4. *(E.C.)*

from Africa who speak (rather it is Orense that speaks),[21] nor by a single monkey's bothersome antics. It is a human tragedy, abject and hellishly human. Especially memorable in it is the acting of Walter Huston, worthy of comparison with the best of Bancroft, the man of the Law of the Underworld and the Docks.

Zoo in Budapest: A film I can honorably recommend but whose omission is not unpardonable—like the dark sin against the Spirit. A pleasingly slow film with good emotional atmosphere that many times rises to the magical. A film that without great difficulty observes the classical unities of time, place, and action. The time: an afternoon, a night, and a morning; the place: the zoo in Budapest; the action: a not disagreeable idyl. A pure film, strengthened and even justified by an excellent photographer.

Die Unsichtbare Front (La flota invisible): Good photography, the greatest and often the only virtue of European films, does not contribute to this production. The plot tries for mystery but does not get beyond being confusing and intolerable. It is so bad that it deserves the signature of René Clair. A happy error in the program says that this is the most impenetrable film that has been shown to date, and it says the truth. I enthusiastically recommend the examination of any other show, even if it is called *King Kong*.

Notes

[21]Capital city of the province in Northwestern Spain with the same name. The allusion is to the thick accent of narrators in the post-synchronized soundtracks of documentaries.

Filmography

KING KONG. U.S.A., 1933. 100 minutes. *Directors and producers*: Merian C. Cooper, Ernest B. Schoedsack. *Original story by* Merian C. Cooper, *adapted by* Edgar Wallace. *Screenplay*: James Creelman, Ruth Rose. *Photography*: Edward Lindon, Vernon L. Walker, J. O. Taylor. *Special effects*: Willis O'Brien. *Cast*: Fay Wray, Robert Armstrong, Frank Reicher, Bruce Cabot. *Produced by* David O. Selznick *for* RKO.

SHE DONE HIM WRONG. U.S.A., 1933. 66 minutes. *Director*: Lowell Sherman. *Screenplay*: Harry Thew, John Bright, *based on the play and with dialogue by* Mae West. *Photography*: Charles Lang. *Cast*: Mae West, Cary Grant, Owen Moore, Gilbert Roland, Noah Berry, Jr. *Producer*: William Lebaron. A Paramount picture.

KONGO. U.S.A., 1932. *Director*: William Cowen. *Screenplay*: Leon Gordon. *Cast*: Walter Huston, Lupe Velez, Conrad Nagel, Virginia Brice, C. Henry Gordon, Mitchell Lewis, Forrester Harvey. An MGM production.

ZOO IN BUDAPEST. U.S.A., 1933. 82 minutes. *Director*: Rowland V. Lee. *Screenplay*: Dan Totheroh, Louise Long, Rowland V. Lee; *based on a story by* Melville Baker, Jack Kirkland. *Photography*: Lee Garmes. *Cast*: Loretta Young, Gene Raymond, O. P. Heggie, Wally Albright, Paul Fix, Murray Kinnell, Ruth Warren. *Produced by* Jesse L. Lasky *for* Fox.

DIE UNSICHTBARE FRONT. Germany, 1932. *Director*: Richard Eichberg. *Screenplay*: Robert A. Stemmle, Max Kimmich, *based on an idea by* Kimmich and Harry Anspach. *Photography*: Bruno Mondi. *Cast*: Karl Ludwig Diehl, Trude von Molo, Alexa von Engström, Jack Mylong-Münz, Theodor Loos, Veit Harlan, Rosa Valetti. *Producer*: Richard Eichberg *for* Film GmbH.

A PROLOGUE*

The two films that make up this book accommodate—or tried to accommodate—the diverse conventions of filmmaking. We were not drawn into writing them with an eye toward innovation. To take up a genre and to make innovations within it seemed excessively rash to us. Predictably, then, the reader of these pages will find the *boy-meets-girl* and the happy ending; or, as has already been said in the letter to the "magnificent and most victorious Lord, the Lord Cangrande della Scala," the *"tragicum principium et comicum finem,"*[22] the perilous reversal and the happy denouement. Quite possibly, such conventions are feeble. In our own case, however, we have noticed how the films that we recall with the greatest emotion—those by von Sternberg and Lubitsch—respect those conventions to no great disadvantage.

These comedies are also conventional in regard to the characters of the hero and heroine. Julio Morales and Elena Rojas, Raúl Anselmi and Irene Cruz, are merely subjects of the action, hollow and pliant forms through which the spectator may pass in order to participate in the incidents. No marked peculiarities stand in the way of one's identification with these characters. One knows that they are young, it is understood that they are attractive, lacking neither in decency nor valor. Let's leave psychological complexity to others. In *Los orilleros* (Men from the River Bank) we leave it for the ill-fated Fermín Soriano; in *El paraíso de los creyentes* (Paradise for Believers), Kubin.

The first film takes place at the end of the 19th century, the second more or less in our own time. Since local and temporal color exist only as a function of differentiation, it is infinitely probable that these qualities will be more noticeable and effective in the first film. In 1951 we know the differentiating characteristics of 1890, but not what in the future will be those of 1951. On the other hand, the present will never seem as picturesque and affecting as the past.

In *El paraíso de los creyentes*, the basic motive is love of money; in *Los orilleros*, emulation. Even though this latter motive suggests morally superior characters, we have resisted the temptation to idealize them, and we believe that neither cruelty nor baseness is lacking

---

*Los orilleros and *El paraiso de los creyentes,* Losada, Buenos Aires, 1955. (E.C.)

in the meeting of the stranger with the boys from Viborita. Of course, both films are romantic, in the same sense that Stevenson's stories are. They are informed by the love of adventure and, perhaps, a distant echo of epics. In *El paraíso de los creyentes,* the romantic tone is emphasized as the action progresses. We have decided that the excitement proper to the ending will smooth over certain improbabilities that might not have been accepted at the beginning.

The theme of the search is repeated in both pictures. Perhaps it is not beside the point to note that in ancient books searches were always successful: the Argonauts captured the Golden Fleece and Galahad the Holy Grail. Nowadays, in contrast, we are mysteriously pleased by the notion of an unending search or of a search for something that, once found, has ruinous consequences. K., the land-surveyor, does not enter the castle, and the white whale destroys the one who eventually finds it. In this sense *Los orilleros* and *El paraíso de los creyentes* do not deviate from the norm of our times.

Contrary to Shaw's opinion that writers ought to flee plots like the plague, we have believed for a long time that a good plot is fundamentally important. The difficulty is that in every complex plot there is something mechanical; the episodes that warrant and explain the action are inevitable and perhaps not spellbinding. Sad to say, the insurance and the ranch in our films correspond to these unfortunate necessities.

As for the language, we have tried to suggest the popular, less by means of vocabulary than by tone and syntax.

In order to make the reading easier, we have shortened or deleted technical terms of *mise-en-scène,* and we have not retained the double-column format.

Up to this point, reader, the logical justification for our work. Yet there are other justifications, of an emotional nature, and we suspect that these latter were more in force than the former. We suspect that the ultimate reason that moved us to imagine *Los orilleros* was the desire to fulfill our obligation, in some way, to certain suburbs, to certain nights and dawns, to the oral mythology of courage, and to the brave, humble music commemorated by guitars.

Jorge Luis Borges and *Adolfo Bioy Casares*
Buenos Aires, 11 December 1951

[22] "And for this reason it is the custom of some writers in their salutation to say by way of greeting: 'a tragic beginning and a comic ending to you!'" *The Letters of Dante,* translated and edited by Paget Toynbee, London, 1920, p. 200.

TWO SYNOPSES OF FILMS

These are the only synopses that Borges agreed to write, in collaboration with Adolfo Bioy Casares, for the original film treatments that Hugo Santiago was to make into movies.

Invasión

Invasión is the story of a city—imaginary or real—besieged by powerful enemies and defended by a few men, who may not be heroes. They fight until the end, without ever suspecting that their battle is endless.

The Others

The son of a Parisian bookseller commits suicide. His father, a man of some fifty-odd years who thought he understood his son, now feels that he never knew him and begins to search for him among the people who had been his friends.

Earlier there had been a masked ball, a film scheduled to be made, a simulated duel, and a poker game that really was a duel. Then, abruptly, death. And then, as the bookseller goes on with his search, more and more unpredictable actions begin to pervade the film.

There is a man who wonders if he is anyone, a magician who says his name is Artajerjes, a woman whom the son had loved, and a forsaken gambler. There is a film scheduled to be made but that is not made, the girl who does not forget the other side of the ocean, and there is an apparition in a procession of horseback riders. There is another man who flings money into the fire and whips the girl for no reason, there is the bookseller who rediscovers love in that girl, and that girl who deceives him with an unknown man who looks like the dead son. And there is a crime in an observatory, and a final revelation:

After the son's death, the bookseller went from being one man to being another, and to being still others. He had no part in these changes; something he did not understand happened to him and led him on. He was the one who wondered if he were someone— the magician who appears and disappears, the violent man who snatched the money away from the gambler and thrashed him, the unknown man who robbed the woman during the night. He stopped being himself in order to be many. Now he can be everybody, and he no longer knows who he is.

FILM ON BORGES

. . . a book whose subject can be all things to all men . . . since it is capable of almost never-ending repetitions, versions, perversions.

"The Life of Tadeo Isidro Cruz," *The Aleph*

Adventures of the Text

It all began in France. If they had not translated my books into French, I think no one would have dreamed of translating them in other countries.

Borges, as reported by Jean de Milleret in *Entretiens avec J.L.B.*, Paris, 1967

A Source for Exegetes

Although literary magazines in the United States, England, and even in France had printed translations of isolated texts by Borges before 1950, his name and work were permanently inscribed in a European intellectual context only starting with the successive French publication of *Fictions* in 1951, *Labyrinthes* in 1953, *Enquêtes* in 1957, and *Histoire de l'infamie* as well as *Histoire de l'éternité* in 1958. While other editions followed these early versions—because Borges's French publishers later tracked down those of his works ripe for translation or promptly welcomed his later books at the same time that studies, homages, and academic theses have proliferated—it is even more curious to note how quoting him, mentioning his name, alluding to one of his titles led the way to securing his position within that space of shared references that traditionally makes up literary culture.

Naturally, this inscription of Borges immediately appeared in French film criticism. Even when paying attention to the most commercial and obscure films, the entrenched Parisians fought in terms of a declared cultural action that even outsiders had to recognize, whether or not they could tell the differences (often dramatized by the adversaries) between *Cahiers du Cinéma*, *Positif*, or *Présence du Cinema*—all factions from the early 60s that constantly invoked Borges while playing at guerilla warfare.

This was a very different situation from what the Spanish language underwent in Latin America. There, even before the Argentine weeklies began imitating his most superficial tics, Borges's diction, syntax, and rhetorical habits had already made available a repertoire of schemes and tropes with which to astonish or censure as well as to enjoy turning the most unassuming or occasional review into literature. Thus, a writer like Guillermo Cabrera Infante, who plays so brilliantly with the literalness and the illusions of language, recognized in G. Cain, the pseudonymous alter ego who signed his film criticism between 1954 and 1960, a taste for literary jokes and erudite fooling, which he practiced "imitating Poe, following in the footsteps of Orson Welles, plagiarizing S. J. Perelman, borrowing from Marcel Schwob, and stealing from Borges." (G. Cain, *Un oficio del siglo veinte*, La

Habana, Ediciones R, 1963; 1973 edition, Barcelona, Seix Barral.) As if to corroborate his statement, Cabrera Infante's introduction announces "a book whose very typography is perverse," which paraphrases the "tower whose very architecture is wicked" that Borges unveiled in his essay "On Chesterton" in *Other Inquisitions*.

France, on the other hand, required the appearance of a film—either *Last Year at Marienbad* by Resnais and Robbe-Grillet, whose cleverly orchestrated ambiguities lend themselves to exegesis even though they do not invite it, or *Paris Belongs to Us* by Rivette, whose less striking oddity provoked a more complex bewilderment—before Borges became a password, a key to a literary space, an impetus for a dizzying chain of connotations to draw a film forward with its own system of references.

(For the sake of accuracy, it is necessary to record that Borges's name first appeared in a French film journal under the guise of a humorous hoax. Paul Louis Thirard published an article entitled "Une question mal connue: les débuts de Maurice Burnam" in *Positif* 13, March-April 1955, and in the filmography for this non-existent director Thirard listed *La marche à la mer*. "The film's rigor, its austerity, derived from an absolute fidelity to Borges's work" were characteristics of an exceptional achievement: "We scarcely recall the astonishment with which the public greeted *La marche à la mer* in 1946." Almost a decade later, another critical hoax was perpetrated by *F for Fake*, a film in which Orson Welles played with notions of truth and falsehood in regard to art. This film was based on interviews with Elmir de Hory, the forger of paintings, and Clifford Irving, author of an apocryphal biography of Howard Hughes that was a *cause célèbre* in its day. In the "Paris Journal," published in *Film Comment* (January-February 1974), Jonathan Rosenbaum proposed that "the new Orson Welles film is co-directed by Irving and de Hory, written by Jorge Luis Borges and produced by Howard Hughes.")

The case of *Last Year at Marienbad* is especially notable since Borges turned up in the wake of Bioy Casares. In an interview with Resnais and Robbe-Grillet conducted by André S. Labarthe and, precisely, Jacques Rivette (*Cahiers du Cinéma* 123, September 1961), the interviewers (Rivette himself perhaps?) venture the hypothesis of a connection between the film and Bioy Casares's

The Invention of Morel. Robbe-Grillet is quick to state that the novel is "an astonishing book" and recounts how, after a private showing of the film, he received a phone call from Claude Ollier, who gasped: "But this is *The Invention of Morel*!" Since Resnais was not familiar with the book, the interviewers told him about those aspects relevant to his film, and the director concluded that the "resemblance was striking." (It is important to recall that when Bioy Casares's novel appeared in France, Robbe-Grillet published a three-page review in *Critique* 69 (February 1953) in which he minutely analyzed the plot, summarized Borges's prologue, and admitted the attractiveness of imagining a "changeable past.") A few pages further into the issue of *Cahiers*, another article ("Dans le dédale" by François Weyergans) points out that Marienbad is mentioned in *The Invention of Morel* and that the apparitions on the island carry on an exchange of weather reports in their conversations. One month later, Ollier began developing his parallel between Resnais's film and Bioy Casares's novel in "Ce soir à Marienbad," which was published in two issues of the *Nouvelle Revue Française* (October and November 1961) and perhaps contributed the best study of the film at the time of its release: neither interpretative nor allegorizing, but, rather, attentive to the effects of connotation and denotation employed by the authors.

The assertion that "The films of Franju resemble the short stories of Borges," can be found in François Tranchant's review of the premiere of *Les Yeux sans Visage* (*Eyes without a Face*, also released in English as *The Horror Chamber of Dr. Faustus*), which appeared in the April issue of *Cinema* 60 (No. 45). Already mentioned in passing by Robert Benayoun in his article "Marienbad, ou les exorcismes du réel" (*Positif* 44, March 1962), Borges, in an epigraph taken from "The Garden of the Forking Paths," also presides over the chapter dedicated to *Last Year at Marienbad* in Roy Armes's book *The Cinema of Alain Resnais* (London, A. Zwemmer, 1968). The author makes use of the system of innumerable and coexistent time frames presented in that story as a model for the narrative structure of Resnais's film and concludes by assigning the following quotation from "The God's Script" to the heroine: "You have not awakened into wakefulness, but into a previous dream. This dream is enclosed within another, and so on into infinity. . . ."

More important, and even earlier, is the case of Rivette's *Paris Nous Appartient* (*Paris Belongs to Us*), whose relation to Borges has an untraceable genealogy. In one of the opening scenes, a copy of *Enquêtes* is seen lying on the heroine's bedside table. In the second part of this section, I will show how this French edition of *Other Inquisitions* got there, but now I want to consider whether or not the critics noticed that appearance, either in the film itself or in the writings of their colleagues.

The first critic to publish his discovery of the book was Paul-Louis Thirard. In an almost disdainful critical essay, which he wrote some time before the film's delayed premiere (*Positif* 35, July-August 1970), Thirard tried to forgive Rivette and his film for their connection with the rival group of *Cahiers du Cinéma*. Aside from that frivolity, the review is far from uninteresting. After beginning with the visible evidence of *Enquêtes* ("Let's try the key: it seems to fit well"), Thirard moves on to *Fictions* and then appraises Rivette according to the assessment Herbert Quain made of his own work. Continuing in a totally Borgesian vein, Thirard then transcribes an apocryphal paragraph that he claims Benjamin Fondane published in *Europe*, about a novel—*L'approche du caché*. Clearly, this non-existent novel is *The Approach to Almotasim*, which Borges invented for his story of the same title, and Thirard identifies the identical device in *Paris Belongs to Us*.

Once again it was Claude Ollier who most significantly developed the connection between Rivette's and Borges's fiction, for the first time when the film premiered. On that occasion, in his review "Finesse et geometrie" for *La Nouvelle Revue Française* 110 (February 1962), Ollier assumed that the exploration of the heroine is secretly influenced by her favorite reading. In turn, this review became the basis for another, less occasional and quite brilliant essay: "Thème du texte et du complot," which is included in the volume *Navettes* (Paris, Gallimard, 1967). There Ollier discerns a paradigm in Borges's "Theme of the Traitor and the Hero" for the working of all narrative, research, and the "appropriation of History by Literature." (It must be pointed out that Ollier pays special attention to the character Nolan, who "changes from being a detective into the impresario of a vast ceremony." This character's name reappears in Ollier's 1967 novel *L'échec de Nolan*, where the device of a detective serves as a metaphor for all narrative. Ollier also imagines the possible development of Nolan's scheme in a film. Without mentioning the title, he describes *Paris Belongs to Us* by paraphrasing the "Theme of the Traitor and the Hero," thereby illustrating his basic proposition about the variable diffusion of narrative in history. Ollier begins his argument:

It is remarkable that a related theme with an analogous concept at its core had already enriched the cinema some years ago. The work was long and dense, woven from multiple episodes. I have not had the opportunity to see it again since its release, and perhaps I have forgotten some points. Certain details, the connections between scenes are gone. Peripheral sections of the story undoubtedly escape my memory. Today, May 13, 1963, I recall it this way: the action takes place in a stubborn, warlike country: Finland, Cuba, some capital coveted by the free world. To clarify the exposition, let's say Paris. Let's say 1958. . . .

Another parallel was drawn by Michel Delahaye in "L'idée maîtresse ou le complot sans maître" (*Cahiers du Cinéma* 128, February 1962) in which he compares Rivette's image of Paris with Feuillade's. (Incidentally, Feuillade's serials come up immediately after *The Invention of Morel* in the previously cited interview with Resnais and Robbe-Grillet, which leads me to assume that of the two interviewers it was indeed Rivette who mentioned them, especially in so far as Feuillade—or, rather, a cinematic notion of serial mysteries embodied by Feuillade—was becoming a reference point for Rivette's most recent work: *Out One Spectre* and the as yet unproduced script of *Phénix*). Similarly, Delahaye draws Fritz Lang's Babel into the comparison (*Paris Belongs to Us* uses a fragment of *Metropolis*) as well as D. W. Griffith's Babylon from *Intolerance*. However, Delahaye concludes that Rivette's Paris "surely ought to be situated at the center of one of Jorge Luis Borges's labyrinthine infernos, where we learn that Babylon lives under the sign of All Powerful Chance: the lottery. But is not chance the form in which the gods' conspiracies express themselves?"

This association of Rivette with Borges was destined to follow an extended career. In order to appreciate its vicissitudes properly, it may be necessary to inform readers unfamiliar with cinematographic literature that in the early 1960s the appearance of the so-called *nouvelle vague* had, among other things, an unexpected and retroactive effect on film criticism outside France. Some talented directors, who simultaneously seemed to alter both the language and the industry of films, had completed their apprenticeship as critics at *Cahiers du Cinéma* or had earned the support of that magazine. At the same time that directors were being promoted from "authors of films" to the category of stars—following the *politique des auteurs* proclaimed by *Cahiers*—and that the job of film critic was acquiring an unheard-of glamour (which in the United States led to a real "star-system"), the label *Cahiers* came to symbolize, rather vaguely, certain trends that received an international sanctification. More than a question of any particular methodology, these trends were a matter of taste, one that flourished simultaneously in the new magazines of various countries, in critical revisions by already established magazines, in a ferment that took some five years to settle before defining a new balance of power, new academies, new vanguards.

One of those magazines, the British *Movie*, tried to develop its own method. In its second issue, September 1962, Borges made his first appearance in English-language film criticism when Paul Mayersberg juxtaposed the first and last sentences of the "The Library of Babel" (not "The Lottery of Babylon" as Delahaye had done) with the first and last sequences of *Paris Belongs to Us*, as an "explanatory parallel." Mayersberg also compared Rivette's Paris with the Library and the protagonist of the film with the "eternal traveller," recognizing in the film's denouement the "elegant hope" with which the narrative concludes: the hope that the "same disorder" repeated "would be an order: the Order." (Like Delahaye, Mayersberg noticed that the play rehearsed but never put on by the theater group is *Pericles*; but neither of them paid attention to the fact that the unfortunate director is named Lenz.)

In a different category altogether came Raymond Durgnat's quaint allusion to the association in the following year (*Nouvelle Vague: The First Decade*, London, A Motion Monograph, 1963). Apparently, Durgnat's reading of Mayersberg suggested to him that "The Library of Babel" is a science fiction novel with a structure analogous to that of *Paris Belongs to Us*.

The passing years, as well as Donald Cammell and Nicholas

Roeg's film *Performance*, would make all this exquisite or borrowed erudition more accessible. In 1962, *Movie* was quoting Borges and going against a British establishment that saw itself represented by *Sight and Sound* and *The Monthly Film Bulletin*, while *Sight and Sound* itself, in a review of *Paris Belongs to Us* (Winter 1961-1962) by Robert Vas contrived a rather obvious literary connection: "This is one of the cinema's nearest equivalents to Kafka." But just a decade later, in the spring issue for 1971, *Sight and Sound* did not scrimp on references to Borges, either in a brief interview with Donald Cammell or, more especially, in Philip French's analysis of *Performance*.

No less interesting are the changing degrees of familiarity with Borges that critics take for granted in their presumed readers: for French, writing in the early 60s, Borges is "the septuagenarian Argentinian author Jorge Luis Borges," while for Jan Dawson, who writes about *Performance* in *The Monthly Film Bulletin* for February 1971, Borges is, simply, Borges. Qualitatively, too, critics became increasingly alert to the presence of Borges in Rivette's and Roeg's work, which had to sustain the long shadow of his influence. In that same fall 1973 issue of *Sight and Sound*, Dawson refers to "Borgesian form" and Tom Milne recognizes a "Borgesian world" in Roeg's *Don't Look Now*. During the same year, the formidable Pauline Kael piled up seven references to Borges in her *New Yorker* piece on the Roeg film (24 Dec. 1973), saying that in "using Du Maurier as a base, Roeg comes closer to getting Borges on the screen than those who have tried it directly." For his part, the tireless Thirard accepted the uncommon talent of Rivette as early as 1974. Writing about *Out One Spectre* in *Positif* 160, Thirard compares the filmmaker with the metaphorical *metteur-en-scène* in "Theme of the Traitor and the Hero" who embodies his fictions in "real" life. The title of Thirard's piece translates one of Borges's: "L'écriture du dieu."

Nevertheless, as early as July 1963, *Cahiers du Cinéma* 145 had reached an extreme where refinement blended with provocation. In that issue Luc Moullet's review of Buñuel's *Exterminating Angel* did not openly allude to Borges yet bore the title, in Spanish, of "Otras inquisiciones." Similarly, in *Présence du Cinéma* 20 (March-April 1964), Jacques Lourcelles entitled a study of Samuel Fuller "Thème du Traître et du Héros" and included an epigraph from the "New Refutation of Time" ("like all men, he was given bad times in which to live"). Lourcelles's concluding paragraph invoked the "the last fifteen lines of the Borges piece about August 23, 1944 that are now becoming as famous as 'The Raven and the Fox'."

In the book review section of the same issue of *Présence* Lourcelles displays his astonishing knowledge of the subject when he launches into the destruction of an article by Goffredo Fofi—"Borges and the Cinema"—that *Positif* had translated in its issue No. 58 (February 1958). Lourcelles's review is, so to speak, an occasion for terrorism between rival magazines. (According to Lourcelles, Fofi "respects the *Positif* tradition, which has always been based on the brotherhood of incompetence and vulgarity.") But Lourcelles's piece is also the testimony of a far from superficial enthusiasm: " . . . in issue 58 one catches a glimpse for the first time of a praiseworthy intention that coincides with one of ours, that is, to publish in French the texts about film written by the Argentine essayist J. L. Borges." (*Positif* followed Fofi's study with Borges's review of *Citizen Kane*). Lourcelles deplores the omissions—Fofi overlooked the volume that includes *Los orilleros* and *El paraíso de los creyentes* along with a revelatory prologue—and the errors—Fofi assumes that SUR is a daily newspaper—as well as the general opinions and the individual attitudes. Although incomplete and less handicapped by errors and omissions than by idle digressions, Fofi's study is nevertheless based on a careful reading of the Borges texts he had within reach. Among his precipitous conclusions—a presumed influence of Borges on Torre Nilsson in *Un guapo de los 1900* and *Fin de fiesta*—Fofi also knows how to detect Borges's link with von Sternberg through the notion of the baroque stated in the prologue to the *Universal History of Infamy*. As for Lourcelles, who remained loyal to the wildest positions of *Présence*, he summarized the year of 1966 in films for the last issue of the magazine (24-25, Fall 1967) by scorning the trends of a so-called "modern cinema" and heading the attack with a quotation from "Funes the Memorious": "My memory, Sir, is like a garbage dump."

Borges enlisted against the new cinema; Borges dragged in to explain that cinema. In the Italian magazine *Cinema & Film*, where literary taste did not exclude either ideological debate or semiology, Luigi Faccini's essay on Glauber Rocha's *Terra em transe* (No. 3, Summer 1967) begins with a quotation from "The

Aleph"—precisely from the same paragraph cited at the beginning of this book, where the narrator explains the difficulty of achieving "even partial enumeration of an infinite whole." For Faccini, " . . . it is not so strange that this sentence by Borges completely defines the philosophical and structural aims of the film." Further on, Glauber Rocha's feverish *mise-en-scène* seems to Faccini "an out-of-focus aleph, infinitely finite . . . within which innumerable, regressive alephs stir." This brief, one-page text does not conclude before linking the "suspension of narrative, naturalistic time and the expansion of the character's mental, metaphysical time" in the film with the similar suspensions and dilations that Borges presents in "The Secret Miracle."

Less unusual, perhaps, than those applied to Rocha, other references to Borges inundate almost every issue of *Cinema & Film*. In No. 10 (Winter 1969-1970), for example, allusions to Borges appear in three separate articles: *(1)* predictably, though subtly, in "El fracaso del arte" (*sic*, in Spanish), an analysis by Franco Ferrini of two Argentine films, Hugo Santiago's *Invasión* and Alberto Fischerman's *The Players vs. ángeles caidos* ("The Players vs. Fallen Angels"); *(2)* in the form of an epigraph taken from "Tlön, Uqbar, Orbis Tertius," and again when the author discusses "The Approach to Almotasim" as a critical method in a study of Hitchcock by Enzo Ungari; *(3)* and, finally, in an opening quotation from "Partial Enchantments of the *Quijote*" from *Other Inquisitions* in Carlo Marletti's review of Bergman's *Shame*.

In France, meanwhile, allusions to Borges had become more and more frequent. As in the case of epithets taken from authors like Kafka and Brecht, the writer's name passed from representing a wider though not very exact frame of reference and ended up by indicating more about the commentator's relationship to one cultural sphere than about the work criticized. Leafing through the issues of *Positif*, for example, one sees that to J.-P. Török the Dutch film *Als Twee Druppels Water* (Like Two Drops of Water) by Fons Rademaker is a "mystery in the manner of both Hitchcock and Borges" (No. 54-55, Report on the Cannes Festival, 1963). In "This Week in Criticism," devoted to the following year's Cannes Festival, the same critic presented a German film, Ferdinand Khittl's *Die Parallel Strasse*, with the proclamation that "Borges finds his most faithful cinematic counterpart in F.

K." (*Positif* 64-65). Later, this film also elicited the epithet "Borgesian" from Robert Benayoun in *Positif* 94 (April 1968).

These examples do not aspire to exhaustiveness; rather, they are intended to illustrate a process. By 1976 it was not only Roeg, predictably enough, with *The Man Who Fell to Earth* but also Francesco Rosi with *Cadaveri eccelenti* who provoked references to Borges—closer to unanimity and insignificance in each instance. An exception to be singled out is Ronald Christ's brilliant essay on *The Man Who Fell to Earth* (published in the *St. Louis Literary Supplement* I:1, November 1976), where Roeg's search for a "new film grammar" is associated with the "assault on our metaphysic, which many of us prefer to call psychology." Roeg's film is read by Christ as having a "metaphysical base" in the literature of, among others, Borges, "who have launched an unremitting attack on the notion of the individual self."

Nor is it surprising that Donald Cammell, making his directorial debut in 1977 with *The Demon Seed* after co-authoring *Performance* with Roeg, should cause the first question asked of Proteus, the computer-robot in the film, to be why the Chinese emperor who constructed the Great Wall also burned all the books. It is equally unsurprising that the answer should repeat an idea expressed in Borges's "The Wall and the Books" from *Other Inquisitions*: there is no contradiction between these actions, which are aspects of the same act. The most obvious risk, however, in citing such illustrative examples is that of composing an inverted image of "The Approach to Almotasim;"—an incessant, interminable dispersion from a once secret source. Like the vestiges of Tlön in this world, the isolated appearances of Borges's imprint establish a network among themselves; they impose an order, sanction a system. For the process to be complete, however, the films themselves, and not just their exegesis, should recapitulate and demonstrate this development.

A Source for Cinéastes

Neither style nor history alone can explain this second process. Perhaps it has been controlled by a circumstantial union of cause and effect: a cultural atmosphere predisposed to the literary practices and the intellectual options of a writer who, translated late and extensively, suddenly appeared in all his splendid peculiarity; a body of film criticism nourished on literature and eager for prestigious results; economic and political conditions that granted certain representatives of that criticism access to production; a cinema that experimented with narrative forms and linguistic practices while simultaneously demanding new critical tools. Hardly successive and superimposed as early as 1960, these phenomena still continue to weave a figure in the carpet.

In Rivette's *Paris Belongs to Us*, the French edition of *Other Inquisitions*, as I mentioned earlier, appears as the heroine's bedside reading, and this is almost certainly the first appearance of Borges in European films, the first link in an unending chain. Worthy of the design in one of Borges's fictions, this appearance was, to a certain degree, the work of chance, as Rivette explained in an interview with Carlos Clarens and myself published in *Sight and Sound* (Fall 1974). Rivette tells there how he had not yet read Borges when he made his first film but how his collaborator Suzanne Schiffman had. Since the book's title—*Enquêtes*—seemed appropriate, a copy was included in one of the first takes, along with a copy of Shakespeare. Later, when critics drew parallels between the film and Borges, Rivette finally read the author whom Schiffman had described to him. Then, in the mid '60s, Rivette tried, unsuccessfully, to adapt "Theme of the Traitor and the Hero," preserving the narrative's multiple levels of fiction and history. Today, he views that attempt as futile because he finds Bertolucci's *The Spider's Strategem* a beautiful film that tells another story in the middle of which "Theme of the Traitor and the Hero" is narrated.

Of course there is also Godard, with his instinct for discovering the least recognizable quotation from an author ("We are all dead men on leave," which in *Breathless* he attributes to Lenin, although Hannah Arendt in her essay on Rosa Luxemburg—*Men in Dark Times*, London, Jonathan Cape, 1970—quotes it as coming from Eugéne Levine, friend of Luxemburg's lover, Leo Jogiches) or for inserting an apparently capricious allusion that lends moving eloquence to the dialogue (Goethe's *Wilhelm Meister* in *La Chinoise*, Rousseau's *Emile* in *Le gai savoir*). But, more important, there is Godard's instinct for incorporating these cultural residues in a structure that, instead of allowing them to accumulate inertly, forces them to collide, thereby increasing their power unexpectedly.

Godard's *Les Carabiniers* is preceded by an insert in which Borges admits, in a conversational tone that suggests the source as an interview: "The further I go, the more I aim at simplicity. I use the most worn-out metaphors because they are eternal: the stars are like eyes . . . , or death, for example, is like sleep." Isolated and printed in that prominent place those words ought to announce the deliberate primitivism that Godard chose as the key to his anti-war fable. If the film is linked to Borges, however, it is not, curiously enough, by any sophisticated desire for simplicity, but, rather, by an aspect that would have left the writer indifferent: its impoverished epic quality, its spun-out absence of heroism. According to Richard Roud, " . . . most war films, however pacifist in intention, cannot avoid scenes which some viewers can take either as glorifications of the warlike spirit or as just plain exciting. Not with *Les Carabiniers*, which successfully re-creates the boredom, the futility, the absolute stupidity of war" (*Godard*, London, Secker and Warburg, 1967). In 1962 Godard could not have been familiar with the reproaches that Borges had directed against the pacifist cinema decades before when writing about *All Quiet on the Western Front* and *The Road Back*, reproaches that could not have prevented the Second World War, but that are still valid for all professional pacifism.

In *Alphaville* (1965) Godard cites Borges again, this time covertly, during the final combat between Lemmy Caution and Alpha 60, the implacable computer that rules the future and provides a scarcely exaggerated image of a Europe where capitalism and socialism have been diluted in a totalitarian common market. In its death throes, the hoarse voice of Alpha 60 spews forth some lines from "A New Refutation of Time": "Time is the substance from which I am made. Time is a river that carries me along, but I am the river; it is a tiger that mutilates me, but I am the tiger; it is a fire that consumes me, but I am the fire."

The same passage, quoted at greater length and printed on a poster along with Borges's signature, closes a less well-known film: *Paris n'existe pas* (1969), the first full-length film by the critic Robert Benayoun. Its protagonist is a painter with an involuntarily retentive memory whose capacity is not limited, as was Funes's, to his individual experience. Living in morose observation of rooms and streets and blocks, he almost archaeologically discovers their previous and, sometimes, their future features.

Another character with a fabulous memory, subjected to a time machine H. G. Wells never dreamed of, is the central figure of *Je t'aime, je t'aime* (1968), directed by Alain Resnais and based on a book by Jacques Sternberg. Resnais, who involuntarily had made the most Borgesian film of all—*Toute la mémoire du monde* (1956)—here used the most obvious science fiction techniques to compose another variation on his favorite theme: the battle between memory and forgetfulness, which ceaselessly redefine the boundaries of their disputed territories. Borges's presence permeates the whole film, and the authors indicate it discreetly in a scene where the protagonist, employed in a publishing house, dictates over the telephone some corrections for proofs that unquestionably belong to a text by or about Borges. Words like "Tlön" or the name "Evaristo Carriego" appear in that scene—a name that is no less fictitious for Europe—as Emir Rodríguez Monegal observed in his prologue to the French edition of *Evaristo Carriego* (Seuil, 1969)—than Herbert Quain or Pierre Ménard.

For years readers and critics recognized Borges by these labyrinths of time and space. Today they are more aware of his skeptical attitude toward the notion of the author, or, more plainly, of identity itself. The Borges of *Performance* and *Les autres* is still the same, but now his readers have also read R. D. Laing or Gilles Deleuze. Before those films, however, a reference in the dialogue of René Allio's *L'une et l'autre* (1967) already belonged to the new series. Just as in *La vieille dame indigne* and *Pierre et Paul*, Allio staged a change of identity in *L'une et l'autre*; but repressive society, which openly had played a part in the process (defeated in the first film, victorious in the second) acts behind the scenes in *L'une et l'autre*, which takes place in a theatrical setting, with an actress as the protagonist. In this film, change itself acquires an almost exemplary capacity. That woman who succeeds in shedding an unsatisfactory identity by representing an ideal one in her "private life" is, of course, a Pirandellian creature. But in a moment of relaxation, while watching a rehearsal from the orchestra, she confesses to a friend that she does not know herself, that perhaps she is like "the unicorn in the Borges story" that no one has seen and no one can be sure of recognizing even if they encounter it. (The allusion is actually to "The Chinese Unicorn," the second of its kind that appears in *The Book of Imaginary Beings*). The interest of this little-known film derives chiefly from its filling an almost naturalistic surface with common, everyday observations, while at the same time constructing a rigorous intellectual base for its traffic in appearances. Instead of weakening the film, this unconcealed polarity, which is sustained throughout, lends *L'une et l'autre* both strength and flexibility, as well as a certain unaffected ambiguity.

Performance responds to the same notion of identity as an assumed role—simultaneously a means of power and a trap—in order to portray the social comedy. Its main characters (a gangster taunted by his accomplices, a pop star fallen into an early decline) undergo violent and erotic turnabouts that are like initiation rites, until each recognizes the other as an alter ego, and they fuse. The film multiplies this game of facing mirrors: the shrill and fleeting scenes of the underworld are the negative image of the asphyxiating decor that protects the rock star, the secondary characters fulfill interchangeable functions, the word "performance" refracts in its multiple meanings (in the arts, in sex, in delinquency, in every exercise of power) a system of correspondences where each small part reproduces the whole design.

Written by Donald Cammell, photographed by Nicholas Roeg, and directed in indistinguishable collaboration by both, this illfated film was made in 1968, filed away by Seven Arts, cut and revamped by Warner, and finally released in 1970 with only marginal, equivocal success. Although it adapted no specific Borges text, *Performance* explicitly derives from all his work (and secondarily from Artaud, Norman O. Brown, and R. D. Laing). Borges appears repeatedly in the film: he crosses the screen twice in jacket photos on identifiable copies of his *Personal Anthology*; he makes himself heard in two quotations that the rock star interpolates in his dialogue (the first quotation from "Tlön, Uqbar, Orbis Tertius," the second from "The South"); and, at the end of the film, his picture emerges from the impact of a bullet fired point blank in the star's face by the gangster—as if at the very instant of being obliterated Mick Jagger's features could free that other, submerged face.

Because of its mixed refinement and brutality as well as its excesses, *Performance* is a cinematic phenomenon inaccessible to literary criteria, even though the film freely incorporates literary material. Perhaps that is its greatest interest: *not* to reflect Borges in an analogous space. Except for Godard, whose work responded to contemporary notions that a Burroughs or a Rauschenberg could handle, the other filmmakers who refer to Borges, with whatever degree of success, do it in intellectual, cultivated, and irremediably polished works. Only *Performance* inoculates the Borgesian element into an organism that functions differently. Even the esoteric quality of the film is not aristocratic; it belongs, instead, to the drug culture, to Hindu bric-a-brac, synthesizer music, bisexuality, and other popularized or tolerated cultural forms of latter-day capitalism. For the spectator with "good taste," it can be irritating and even incomprehensible, as John Simon demonstrated in a rather lengthy attack: ". . . even that great writer, Jorge Luis Borges, is dragged into the cesspool. . . . It is all mindless intellectual pretension and pathologically reveled-in nastiness, and it means nothing" ("The Most Loathsome Film of All?", *The New York Times*, 23 August 1970).

Formerly a man of the theater, Carmelo Bene presents a very special case of a filmmaker who proclaims his familiarity with Borges, given that his films neither derive from nor coincide with Borges's writings. Instead, Bene invokes Borges as an argument within a polemic that proceeds according to the most excessive and disparate styles of theatrical presentation—chiefly grand opera but also the circus, as well as certain esthetics of North American underground cinema—in order to fight the provincialism of Italian culture and, at the same time, to define its authentic traditions. In the polyglot soundtrack of *Don Giovanni* (1970), for example, Bene inserts a sentence from "Tlön, Uqbar, Orbis Tertius": "Copulation and mirrors are abominable because they multiply the number of living things." Originally, Borges put these words into the mouth of Bioy Casares, who in turn attributed them to an encyclopedia of questionable existence. In Bene's film, however, they are pronounced, in their hypothetical English, about the image of the protagonist and author who throws himself against a mirror and disappears among its broken pieces.

In such a context, Borges is used merely to indicate a cultural milieu, just as he is when Jean-Pierre Léaud quotes him inexactly in Jean Eustache's *La maman et la putain* (1973). Like the name of F. W. Murnau, the voices of Zarah Leander and Damia, the Café de Flore, and the restaurant at the Gare de Lyon, the allusion to Borges in Eustache's film figures as a sign or symptom of a particular taste or attitude.

The gloss on "New Refutation of Time" in Shuji Terayama's *Pastoral Hide and Seek* has an equivalent value. In this film, memory is the game of hide and seek, and the narrator, who seeks his own identity, wonders: "Borges says: the coin lost five days ago and the one we find today are not the same. How, then, can we suppose that this coin existed yesterday and the day before yesterday?"

A marginal note to this inventory ought to indicate that in 1970 Jean-Marie Straub used Borges's essay "On Dubbing" to defend his film *Othon*, which Italian Radio-Television, as co-producer, wanted to dub for showing in Italy. Straub published his repudiation of this attempt in several periodicals, tracing the genealogy of dubbing as an authoritarian instrument and quoting Borges extensively. Valid for all cinema, Straub's reasoning provoked amazement at the bureaucratic logic behind the notion of dubbing any of his films, not just this one, whose complete title is *Les yeux ne veulent pas en tout temps se fermer, ou Peut-être qu'un jour Rome se permettra de choisir à son tour*. RAI obviously lost sight of the fact that it was sponsoring a director whose films employ direct sound—including all its possiblities for the unpredictable—as significant material. Furthermore, in *Othon* the interplay of foreign accents violating the accepted way of declaiming Corneille's metrics furnishes a major element in the reading of the film's tragedy—like the interplay between classical Rome, as presented in the actors' costumes, and a modern-day Rome, visible as well as audible in the background of both the visual image and the soundtrack.

Versions and Perversions

DÍAS DE ODIO

DÍAS DE ODIO (Days of Hatred), 1953-1954. 66 minutes. *Director:* Leopoldo Torre Nilsson. *Screenplay:* Jorge Luis Borges, Leopoldo Torre Nilsson. *Based on "Emma Zunz," a story by* Jorge Luis Borges. *Photography:* Enrique Wallfisch. *Music:* J. Rodríguez Fauré. *Editing:* Rosalino Caterbetti. *Producer:* Armando Bo. *Cast:* Elisa Christian Galvé (Emma), Nicolás Fregues (Plessner), Raúl del Valle (sailor), Duilio Marzio (boy in the park), Enrique de Pedro, Virginia Romay, Lina Bardo, Luis Belti, José Guisone, José María Fra, Carmen Giménez, Elida Dey, Leonor Barret, Angel Prío, Lois Blue, Pepe Soriano, Héctor Bianciotti. A SIFA production.

Borges did not like this first film adaptation of one of his texts, and he did not miss any opportunity to make his displeasure known. The film's faults are obvious, but they matter less than its good points. Upon completing the film, Torre Nilsson himself stated that he had planned for *Días de odio* to last, ideally, only twenty-five minutes ("Historia de una película," *Gente de cine* 29, Buenos Aires, January-February 1954); but the three-part film he intended it for was never made, so the script had to be expanded into a feature-length film. Consequently, it became necessary to invent additional scenes and these blurred the story's linear pattern, or, more precisely, its "effect of linearity" since a careful reading reveals a constant interplay among the story's various levels. As for Borges, he collaborated closely with the director in writing the script and did not object to having his name included in the credits.

Without either favoring fidelity to its literary source or disdaining the movie industry's conventions, one still feels that the film would benefit from the elimination of its "romantic interest," of the couple's encounter in a wintry park—conceived as a counterpart to their loneliness—that culminates when they escape from a noisy birthday party by taking refuge in a kitchen. Similarly, the film would benefit from the cutting of its "comic relief": a colorful tough, who, in the purely verbal context, say, of "The Intruder" may appear an acceptable archetype, but who cannot hold up under the film's precise observation of his battered, broad-brimmed hat, his silk handkerchief, wrinkles, and whiskey voice. Still, these distractions are well thought out according to a classical model of narrative construction that defines character by means of incidental situations that establish the basis for later development. For example, Emma's hesitant contact with a melancholy suitor illustrates her sexual timidity, which is crucial to the credibility of her alibi and her gruesome vengeance, while the tough's protecting her lets Emma glimpse a kind of night-life that becomes part of her plan. The film also invents good sequences, such as the anonymous funeral cortege that Emma follows when she cannot attend her own father's funeral, and these inventions seem equally as characteristic of the writer as of the director. (In his 1956 film *El Protegido*, for which he alone wrote the script, Torre Nilsson had planned to include a brief, isolated flashback to the fiction created by the characters, who are movie people, from their fictitious "real life." Today, critics would call that moment "Borgesian.")

Some thirty years after the fact, it is even more interesting to take note of what Torre Nilsson attempted in this his first full-length film (excluding, of course, *El crimen de Oribe*, 1950, based on Bioy Casares's "El perjurio de la nieve," which he co-directed with his father, Leopoldo Torres Ríos). Nothing in the Argentine cinema of its time resembles *Días de odio*. In 1953, only Bresson's *Diary of a Country Priest* and Astruc's *Le rideau cramoisi* (*The Crimson Curtain*) had tried to relate a highly literary story, told on the soundtrack, with a plot reduced almost entirely to a single character. In Torre Nilsson's experiment, the infrequent gestures, the frames chosen to emphasize rather than mask the absence of conventional drama, the extremely rich soundtrack—where a radio has been left playing and Emma hears it on reviving from a faint, or where the wind rustles clotheslines in a hotel patio for hours on end—indicate the kind of work with film language that attracted the director. *Días de odio* revealed Torre Nilsson's sense of his medium, which would grow even sharper in his later films but had already begun to emerge with all the impatience and boldness of every first work.

On the other hand, the story's paradoxical relationship between truth and verisimilitude mattered less to Torre Nilsson than did the character's loneliness, from which Torre Nilsson derived his own emotional attitude toward the film. "As the film began to take shape in my mind, it started to take on a meaning of its own," the director explained in the article already cited. "At that point, 'Emma Zunz' stopped being the story of a girl seeking a perfect way to avenge her father's disgrace and death. It became the story of solitude opposed to community. In *Días de odio* I tried to show more than the reversals of plot and psychology; I tried to show the repetitive counterpoint of man and society." From this premise Torre Nilsson derived his diligent elaboration of the plot's secondary action, so that situations occasionally take on suffficient density to cover up the cast's deficiencies. The transformation of Buenos Aires into an ambience defined by a single character also derives from that premise: even though Emma's isolation is motivated novelistically, her solitary pilgrimage, which today seems to anticipate Antonioni's passive heroines, is set in a hostile city, a humiliating factory, a room in a depressing boarding house. This romantic pessimism also proved unusual in Argentine films of the Peronist period, which had been indifferently optimistic, vigorously ineffectual. By way of contrast, the film produced a realistic effect, subsequently eroded, while the "will to style" impressed on every aspect of the film remains undiminished.

HOMBRE DE LA ESQUINA ROSADA

HOMBRE DE LA ESQUINA ROSADA (Man on the Pink Corner). Argentina, 1961-1962. 70 minutes. *Director:* René Mugica. *Screenplay:* Joaquín Gómez Bas, Isaac Aisemberg, Carlos Aden. *Based on the story by* Jorge Luis Borges. *Photography:* Alberto Etchebehere. *Music:* Tito Ribero. *Sets:* Gori Muñoz. *Editing:* Jorge Garate. *Sound:* Ricardo Brovell. *Dialogue recording:* Mario Fezia. *Camera:* Ricardo Agudo. *Make-up:* Vicente Notari. *Hairstyles:* Susana Fernández. *Still photography:* Miguel Guglielino. *Head of production:* Adolfo Cabrera. *Cast:* Francisco Petrone, Susana Campos, Walter Vidarte, Jacinto Herrera, Juan Carlos Galván, Berta Ortegosa, Ricado Argeni, Jorge de la Riestra, Mario Sabino, Manuel Rosón, María Esther Podestá, María Esther Buschiazzo, Adolfo Linvel, Alberto Barcel, Tino Pascali, Isidro Fernán Valdez, Eduardo Bergara Leumann, Andrés Ernesto Ribero. An Argentina Sono Film production.

In his 1954 prologue to a new edition of *Universal History of Infamy*, Borges wrote that "The Man on the Pink Corner" (or "Streetcorner Man" as Norman Thomas di Giovanni and Borges later translated it in *The Universal History of Infamy*, New York, 1972) "has enjoyed a singular, somewhat mysterious success." The "belabored composition," which Borges also referred to in that preface, seems to have been governed solely by his interest in staging a tableau of purely verbal local color, in pursuing an imaginary philology, even of playing with a first-person narrative whose authority is called into question at the end by the sudden appearance of a second speaker: that same "Borges" to whom the story has been deceptively addressed. That such a frankly artificial story could have appeared to many critics as Borges's rare venture into realism reveals a misconception similar to the error of confusing "Emma Zunz," that game based on the nature of narrative probability, with a sort of combined detective story and slice of life. "Streetcorner Man" is the Borges story preferred by those readers least interested in his writing. It is possible to discover in it a certain folkloric picturesqueness, a surprise ending, a hasty marriage of passion and death that guarantee the tale's effectiveness. Frequently, nothing more has been discovered in it.

The film based on that story, however, discovers other possibilities. Made in 1962 by Argentina Sono Film to increase that company's prestige, the film tried to reconcile the name of a famous writer (who by that time occupied a position of honor in the *ecclesia visibilis* of Argentine letters very different from the one he held when *Días de odio* was made) with some opportunities for spectacle. The adapters pushed back the time of the action to May 25, 1910, so that all the excitement of the nation's centennial would dominate the slim plot. Street dancing, folk races, tugs of war, and greased poles are some of the "numbers" that enliven the film. More importantly, the studied brevity of the dialogue as well as the ability on the part of René Mugica to link episodes with their setting confer a highly professional stamp on the enterprise. According to the categories that still retained some usefulness when these films were made, *Días de odio* was looked at as a pure example of "author's cinema," while *Hombre de la esquina rosada* offered an equally clear example of a genre film.

As for Mugica, he approached the film according to his own ideas. In Francesco Real he saw "a character with an enormous capacity for tragedy . . . a very typical person in my country. For a long time they have lived with the tragic destiny of killing without even knowing their victims. They have had to kill people they met only a little while before. They have had to endure this tragedy until they themselves are killed or until they are destroyed. . . . I tried to say through them that *machismo* is worthless, that a man's values cannot be based on that conception of life. Neither can love be reduced to that" (quoted by José Luis Egea, *Nuestro cine* 14, Madrid, November 1962).

The purpose behind Mugica's criticism corresponded to the intention of those U.S. film makers who set out to dissect genres, like the western, or types, like the gangster, from within, so as to expose their ideological base. What severely limits this aspect of Mugica's film is not so much the acceptance of another set of rhetorical conventions (in the acting, dramatic situation, and lighting) as the tendency to replace those archetypes with figures from classical tragedy, eliminating the very individuals who embody them and whom the director recalls in his statements. This same tendency prevailed in Mugicas's next film—*El reñidero* (1963)—where, following the pattern of a successful play by Sergio de Cecco, he transcribed situations out of Sophocles, using the local color of a turn-of-the-century Buenos Aires neighborhood.

INVASIÓN

INVASIÓN (Invasion). Argentina, 1968-1969. *Director:* Hugo Santiago. *Screenplay:* Jorge Luis Borges, Hugo Santiago, *based on an original idea by* Jorge Luis Borges *and* Adolfo Bioy Casares. *Photography:* Ricardo Aronovich; *additional photography:* Adelqui Camusso; *camera:* Enrique Filipelli; *assistants:* Roberto Macari, Bebe Latour. *Music and sound:* Edgardo Cantón; *song:* "Milonga de Manuel Flores" (Aníbal Troilo-Jorge Luis Borges) *by* Ubaldo de Lío *(guitar) and* Roberto Villanueva *(vocal)*. *Editing:* Oscar Montauti; *assistant:* Alberto Yaccelini. *Sets and costumes:* Leal Rey; *art designer:* Juan Romano; *wardrobe:* Julia Malfetani. *Titles:* Juan Carlos Distefano; *map of Aquilea:* Hugo Scornik. *Makeup:* Oscar Combi. *Hair styles:* Susana Moccagato. *Head of production:* Luis César Giudice; *manager:* Juan Pallí. *Deputy producer:* Hugo Santiago. *Cast:* Lautaro Murúa (Julián Herrera), Olga Zubarry (Irene), Juan Carlos Paz (Don Porfirio), Martín Adjemian (Irala), Daniel Fernández (Lebendiger), Roberto Villanueva (Silva), Oscar Cruz (Leader of the Southerners), Jorge Cano (Julio Vildrac), Ricardo Ormellos ("Cachorro"), Leal Rey (Moon), Horacio Nicolai (an invader), Juan Carlos Galván (leader of the invaders), Aldo Mavo (leader of another group of invaders), Hedy Krilla (old servant), Claudia Sánchez (woman in the restaurant), Edgardo Lusi (defender of the Southerners), Oscar Espíndola, Aldo Barbero, and Raúl del Valle (invaders of the island). Luis M. de la Cuesta (Miguel), María de los Angeles Medrano (girl with puma), Bernardino Ropero (old man in the café), Karen (woman with the invaders), Norma Hummel (Lebendiger's friend), Rafael Salvatore (Cesáreo), Luis Mathé (murderer of Moon and Lebendiger), Hugo Santiago (driver), Ricardo Aronovich (man at target practice). A Proartel production.

Like Brecht's *In the Jungle of the Cities* and Losey's *Men in a Landscape*, *Invasión* presents a story whose motivation remains concealed. In some notes for a new edition of his early works, included in *Writings on Theater*, Brecht recalls his concern with staging a fight for the sake of the fight itself: a rigorous, self-sufficient mechanism like that of a boxing match. This concern made him pay renewed attention to the smallest details of the action, to the substance and color of the words epitomizing the conflict. While working on his problem, he corroborated the special complexity of literary creation: "form" and "content"—those pittances of the critic, those hindsight mirages of the reader—disappeared in an endless, creative interaction among simultaneous aspects of a single work.

In the theater, words may take on exceptional vigor if the omission of logical motives for dramatic action enhances them, if they must serve as the rationale for actions overturning all the demands of naturalistic verisimilitude. The information withheld from the audience blots out the transparency of the language, turning it into a solid, luminous surface not meekly yielding to being a vehicle. Films, instead, do not allow similar possibilities for cutting away: every contingent element of the image produces an effect of connotation as inevitable as it is difficult to control. In *Men in a Landscape* it is not enough to conceal the crime committed by the fugitives, the suffering they have fled, even the country that serves as the setting for their flight. Stripped of every informative connection, any inkling of the past, the mere physical presence of the actors as well as their gestures and tone immediately suggest various possible contexts. The resulting paradox—valid in the theater too, but less intensely there—is that these mechanisms, reduced to their plainest function, assume hypothetical significance: an example of the *horror vacui* that Henry James shrewdly foresaw in stories where a central ellipsis sustains complex narrative architecture and hurls the reader into the game of interpretation.

Invasión takes place in a city that does not exist outside the film. Its name—Aquilea—resonates with a certain mythological connotation, while its city plan, shown at various times during the film, is a stylized version of the layout of Buenos Aires. The city's visible topography is that of Buenos Aires as well, but with vast sections omitted and the remainder grouped in unexpected neighborhoods and arrangements. The city explored by the film is like shorthand for more complex, missing signs; yet, at the same time, the film provokes a double shock of recognition and surprise in people who know Buenos Aires. It would not be inappropriate to compare this city to the urban counterfeit in "Death and the Compass."

All that is known about this city is that invaders and defenders fight over it in an undeclared war consisting of skirmishes that prepare for the final resolution in occupation and resistance. Impatient to discover an allegorical meaning in this action, whose causes are hidden, the audience is defeated by contradictory information. The most misleading clue is the date, 1957, which appears next to the name Aquilea at the start of the film. According to the authors, this date was chosen because it is not open to interpretation and, at the same time, thwarts those who might point to the absence of a precise time.

Nevertheless, even though Borges, Bioy Casares, and Santiago deny it, *Invasión* has been accumulating *a* meaning ever since it was filmed, with the course of subsequent history perhaps coloring the purely fictive object that the film attempted to be. That resolutely gray city, those characters who cultivate a stoical tight-lip, might be components of the "hard-boiled" novel before being cheapened by the *série noire*, but they are also the circumstances of the *porteño*, the citizen of Buenos Aires, who is defeated in advance and inherits a discredited tradition. As the film progresses, the dark clothing, the lonely sipping of maté, the tender, ripping sound of the accordion become signs for a way of life capable of being idealized (that is, where a seed of myth can be found) to the same degree that it accepts being condemned, as a proud, liberal city, to remaining on the fringes of history—left, like Alexandria or Trieste, to a splendid or obscure extinction. The invaders, with their white clothes, definite gestures, and sparsely furnished offices triumph, just as a race of technocrats can triumph over a handful of sportsmen, just as the notion of efficiency destroys the idea of fair play. The groups of young people who have appeared occasionally during the film become the resistance movement and take charge of the fight, but "in our own way." This last sequence is the most noteworthy. It appears after the phrase "The End," and its successive dissolves superimpose almost identical images from minimally different angles, producing two important effects: *(1)* an indefinite multiplication of the number of youths who take up arms for the fight, and *(2)* a violation of cinematic "grammar," which has been respected up to that point. In every sense, this portion situates itself outside the film, and beyond its laws, in a human, narrative, cinematic, ideological space that is totally *other*.

Interpretation may be irresistible, but it is certainly unnecessary in order to appreciate a film whose meticulous production affects every level, posing continually different oppositions: gaps that serve to punctuate what is basically an action film; snatches of tangos and milongas on a soundtrack composed like a score for concrete music; natural sources of lighting in a film that unemphatically scorns all naturalism; concise and definitive dialogue, like that in sagas, between characters whose heroism has overcome their modern, urban condition in the first place. All of which gives rise to a play of tension and release that equally determines the narrative order and the *mise-en-scène*, alternating brief and intensely violent acts with delicate or ominous pauses. In a word: cinema.

Like its characters, who do not mean to please but to play—elegantly and honorably—a game whose rules are demonstrated in the very act of obeying them, *Invasión*—difficult and proud—imposes itself on the viewer. The film offers itself as a stage where different conceptions of the cinema, which in theory should be mutually exclusive, confront each other—Walsh and Bresson, for example. Far from destroying each other, their encounter produces a severe, complex, intelligent cinematographic object—unavailable to either allegory or sequential narrative—that grants itself the luxury of achieving a closed form of perfection only to violate it in its final minute.

EMMA ZUNZ

EMMA ZUNZ. France, 1969. 54 minutes. *Direction and screenplay:* Alain Magrou. *Based on the story by* Jorge Luis Borges. *Photography (Eastmancolor):* Daniel Vogel, Jean-Luc L'Huillier. *Music:* François de Roubaix. *Editing:* Image de France, Walter Spohr, Patrice de Bruchard. *Sound:* Severin Frankel; *Mixing:* Christian Forget. *Production assistant:* Bernard Bolzinger. *Still photography:* Francis Gourot. *Producers:* Pierre Kafian, Alain Magrou. *Cast:* Catherine Salviat (Emma), Michel Etchevery (Löwenthal), Marianik (Perla), Théo Fouquet and Francis Bernard (Perla's friends). *Dialogue coach:* Philipe Avron. A Coprocine-Les Films Alain Magrou film in association with the Société C. Chevereau.

Produced for French television, this second adaptation of "Emma Zunz" had a clear advantage from the start: meant to last less than an hour, it did not have to stretch out the story with unnecessary digressions. The resulting film, however, was so weak, so approximative, that a great part of its reduced footage is repetitive or merely ineffective. Moreover, the entire adaptation seems to have been overwhelmed by a brief passage at the end of the story's second paragraph: "She picked up the piece of paper and went to her room. She furtively put it away in a box, as if somehow she already knew the subsequent events. Perhaps she had already begun to glimpse them: she already was the person she would become." From these few lines arose the unfounded assembling of a long sequence of premonitory images based on the moment when Emma, standing in front of her window, crumples the letter informing her of her father's death. These staccato flashes-forward are poorly edited, arranged with no interesting cinematic idea to support them. They induce sleep rather than excite suspense, and their avalanche of clues, more irritating than alarming, promises no ultimate revelation.

Except for the notable presence of Cathérine Salviat, who provides Emma with a shy face and is able fight off the monotony of the scheme that Magrou has laid out for her, and except for the exterior shots of Marseilles, which contrast the summery, crowded, foreign liveliness of the city with the story of a private vengeance, this is an utterly forgettable film.

STRATEGIA DEL RAGNO

STRATEGIA DEL RAGNO (*The Spider's Strategem*). Italy, 1969-70. 97 minutes. *Director:* Bernardo Bertolucci. *Screenplay:* Marilú Parolini, Eduardo de Gregorio, Bernardo Bertolucci. *Based on the story "Theme of the Traitor and the Hero" by* Jorge Luis Borges. *Photography (Eastmancolor):* Vittorio Storaro, Franco di Giocomo. *Music: excerpts from* Verdi's *Rigoletto; the song "The Conformist" by* Mina and Martelli, *sung by* Mina. *Editing:* Roberto Perpignani. *Sound:* Giorgio Pelloni. *Sets and costumes:* María Paola Maino. *Head of production:* Aldo V. Passalacqua. *Producer:* Giovanni Bertolucci. *Cast:* Giulio Brogi (Athos Magnani), Alida Valli (Draifa), Pippo Campanini, Franco Giovannelli, Tino Scotti. An RAI-Red Film production.

Perhaps no other literary text has offered itself so provisionally to its eventual adapters as "The Theme of the Traitor and the Hero," which is the point of departure for Bertolucci's *The Spider's Strategem*: " . . . I have imagined the plot for a story that I may write someday and that somehow already justifies my idle afternoons. The details, emendation, adjustments are missing, and there are portions of the story as yet unrevealed to me. This is how I see it today, January 3, 1944. . . ." Borges even went on to invite diverse translations of the story: "The action takes place in an oppressed, dogged country: Poland, Ireland, the Republic of Venice, some South American or Balkan state. . . . Let's say (for narrative convenience) Ireland; let's say 1824."

Bertolucci and his script writers—an Argentine and an Italian—said Italy, said the 1930s; but *Strategem* fits into no historical genre. The film is neither a cast-of-thousands spectacular nor a contemporary interpretation of past times and events; rather, it is, more than anything else, a film about the continuity of past and present, about their connection and interaction. In Borges's story, the central character Ryan is the grandson of one Kirkpatrick, a martyr of the Irish rebellion, while in Bertolucci's film, the main character, Athos Magnani, is the son of Athos Magnani, a hero of the anti-Fascist resistance. As in *The Conformist*, which he made immediately after *Strategem*, Bertolucci does not see Fascism as a historic development that is over and done with but as a system of attitudes and behavior in which ideology grows stronger in inverse proportion to its explicit manifestation. In *The Conformist*, the family's lunch or the vast governmental architecture *are* Fascism; in *Strategem*, the movements with which the elder Athos dances to "Giovinezza" before the townspeople *are* defiant opposition.

The elder Athos Magnani was a coward trapped within a romantic conception of political action, at once heroic and ingenuous. (Better than any scene in the film, the name of his lover, the daughter of a bitter Dreyfusard, illustrates this concept: her father has baptized her Draifa.) For such partisans, the only popular cultural tradition that can match the staging of a Shakespearian play in Borges's story is a Verdi opera, whose historic Risorgimento atmosphere is as appropriate to their militance as to their countryside. (The film was shot in the Po Valley, between Mantua, the setting of *Rigoletto*, and Parma, Bertolucci's native city; to be more exact, in Sabbioneta, a model of Renaissance city planning whose almost abstract mass and geometric perspectives nowadays evoke de Chirico.) Thus the staging of *Julius Caesar* is replaced by a production of *Rigoletto*; and, consequently, the "ides of March" motif is lost, but the theme of the son murdering his father is gained. For the adapter's concept of the plot, this theme is much more important than the classical allusion.

To Bertolucci, the film resembles psychoanalytic therapy. He explains that in the original story "the cyclic echoing of events, which is very Borgesian, didn't attract my attention. The theme of the film really is a kind of trip to the kingdom of the dead. . . . The investigation conducted by the young man is like a trip through atavistic memory, through the pre-conscious ("Conversation with Bertolucci," *Filmcritica* 209, Rome, September 1970). As a result, the political and ideological continuity of past and present assumes a new dimension. Bertolucci makes the same actor play both father and son, places these characters in similar situations, and renders Draifa's reactions ambiguous. (Does she take the son for the father at one point? Does the resemblance between the father and son awaken her old love? Did the tender scene with the fainting son perhaps take place in the past with the father?) Furthermore, with very brief shots of running legs and others of agitated bodies and heads that successively identify father and son, Bertolucci composes an alternating montage for the escape of each, thirty years apart, through the same forest. Draifa's role is the most eloquent element in this series: Circe or Medusa, she has summoned the son, and through her the "kingdom of the dead" works its most palpable spell. Her confusion of generations—as trivial as a symptom of old age—sets forth the film's central subject: the defeat of Athos.

Strategem displays a very special cross-section of ideological, esthetic, as well as psychoanalytic planes, and the cutting occurs in the most unpredictable way, obliquely revealing the levels' extension and discovering their unusual outlines and volumes. The son desecrates the father's tomb, but his rage is no liberation, no total profanation, because he acts it out before learning the truth. Precisely at the moment when he discovers that truth, he is trapped in the same lie sanctioned by the whole society. This unraveling of the plot lends the film a certain ideological pathos since, in order to conceive of history as the story of what really happened, it is necessary to reject myth, even though mythology may better inform history than some insignificant speck of documented truth. Unlike the John Ford of *The Man Who Shot Liberty Valance*, in which the lawman accepts the supremacy of the brave man and allows myth to occupy the stage of history, Bertolucci works in a context where a similar paradox would be unacceptable. To the degree that *Strategem* presumes a meditation on the persistence of Fascism ("Fascism will continue; Fascism is already inside the people") as well as on the contemporary history of Italy, the retort from Brecht's *Galileo*, which Bertolucci quoted during the filming, is apt: "Pity the country that needs heroes. . . ." (In the play, Galileo posed that aphorism against Andrea Sarti's earlier one: "Pity the country with no heroes." Deferring to the Inquisition, Galileo has recanted, and he knows that his "betrayal" will be more useful than the integrity of a naive idealist who is impatient to sacrifice his life for his ideas.)

Moreover, Bertolucci was wise enough to admit in the previously cited interview: "Of course I say all this now, and I did think about it before starting to shoot, but that doesn't have anything to do with anything. I mean, psychoanalysis is psychoanalysis, and films are films . . . and I'm not at all interested in making psychoanalytic films." The truth is that this trip to the "kingdom of the dead" uncovers two parental images: one of the father, the hero/traitor/hero, and one of the "mother," an attractive, dangerous figure who is the instrument of that second intrigue which is the disclosure and acceptance of the first. Instead of freeing him, the knowledge that the traveller achieves destroys him. In Borges's story, Ryan takes positive satisfaction in accepting his predecessor's scheme, in submitting to the design already sketched by history; in Bertolucci's film, that resolution implies defeat.

Various foreshadowings in the film predict this defeat: the camera focuses in on the father's statue so that its bulk shrouds the son; Draifa dresses the young man in his father's clothes; the presentation of *Rigoletto*, the *mise-en-scène* of the ostensible conspiracy in the present and the real conspiracy in the past, governs, from ubiquitous loudspeakers, the son's impossible escape. As in classic tragedy as well as in psychoanalytic investigation, the film presents an unhurried yet inevitable linking of clues and revelations. For example, the train is delayed, first for forty minutes, then for two hours. A skeptical station master observes that sometimes the train forgets to pass through at all. A travelling shot, the last shot in the film, gradually reveals the grass, growing progressively higher between the railroad tracks.

This confrontation takes place in a transfigured setting. Behind the opening credits, a naive painting, *The Flight of the Lion in the Forest of Poplars* by Ligabue, establishes a tone, both for the cornfields drenched in sun and the too luxuriant vegetation invading Draifa's garden. Even the architecture of Sabbioneta evokes not only de Chirico but also Delvaux and finally Magritte in night scenes filmed without compensation so that the existing electric lights bring out violently orange areas under an intensely blue sky—a contrast between "natural" and "artificial" illumination that Vittorio Storaro repeated in *The Conformist* and *Last Tango in Paris*. No scrap of "nature" in the film escapes underscoring or absorption by this calligraphy, even when it is not a matter of erudite pictorial references but only an incidental touch of color, such as what a red handerchief lends to a landscape or a bunch of flowers and some slices of watermelon give to a white tablecloth.

This treatment works like a varnish, both preserving and distancing the action under a glaze that defines it all with a certain emblematic, atemporal quality. Thus Bertolucci establishes a tension with the elements of local color, even of naturalism, that he introduces into the film. This local color—wrinkled faces of the villagers, a boy reciting Pascoli, people drinking wine outdoors—can undergo a sudden allegorical transformation: the women wearing black, crowding into motionless wagons in the night, absorbed in listening to Verdi's music broadcast over the loudspeakers proclaiming to the young Athos the omens that announced the death of his father.

This technique may be compared to the one Bertolucci employed in his first film, *La commare secca* (*The Grim Reaper*, 1962). There, the remnants of neo-realism on which the plot turns appear in quotation marks, like cultural documentation. For example, the hysterical outburst of a girl in a kitchen, suddenly filled with neighbors who have come to calm her, is a bit of melodrama included as information, since the different accents and dialects define the many episodic characters. In *Strategem* the sweeping, majestic movements of the camera bestow an operatic emphasis on scenes whose action is not, in itself, grand. One sequence that illustrates this treatment occurs when Athos the son visits the manufacturer of *culatelle*, one of the men who conspired with the elder Athos. Like alternating stanzas, their conversation interweaves thoughts about the art of curing hams and the necessity of fighting against Fascism, along with quotations from *Ernani* and *A Masked Ball*—all between rhythmic fade-ins and fade-outs that take on the quality of caesurae.

Another aspect that Bertolucci develops in a minor way is the notion of film as collective memory, an idea that the director, like many of his contemporaries, enjoys illustrating. For example, the white figure of the sailor, who arrives in town on the same train as the son and reappears in the last sequence, is a ghost of the protagonist from *La commare secca*, played by the same Allen Midgette, while the name Bertolucci chooses for the locale is Tara, which does not sound foreign to the region but, of course, comes from the classic *Gone with the Wind*.

The concept of universal history as a story or metaphor written by diverse characters who, in turn, are written by it, a concept that Borges derived from the Scholastics through Bacon, is here associated with an unexpected echo. In the eulogy that he is obliged to give in honor of his father, young Athos says: "One man is equal to all men, is as good as all men, and all men are equal to him." According to Bertolucci (interviewed in *Sight and Sound*, Spring 1971) this quotation comes from Sartre, but in the context of the film it seems to be lifted out of *El Hacedor* (*Dreamtigers*.) Young Athos, prisoner and leader of the plot he has discovered, remains paralyzed: "Whoever has glimpsed the universe, whoever has glimpsed the passionate designs of the universe, can no longer think about only one man, about his trivial joys and miseries, even if he is that man himself. *He has been that man, and now he does not matter anymore*" ("The God's Script," *The Aleph*).

LES AUTRES

LES AUTRES (The Others). France, 1973-74. 130 minutes. *Director:* Hugo Santiago. *Based on an original story by* Jorge Luis Borges, Adolfo Bioy Casares, Hugo Santiago. *Photography (Eastmancolor):* Ricardo Aronovich. *Music and sound structures:* Edgardo Cantón. *Editing:* Alberto Yaccelini. *Sets and costumes:* Antonio Seguí. *Mixing:* Jean-Pierre Turolla. *Camera:* Bernard Noisette; *first assistant cameramen:* François About, Daniel Leterrier; *second assistant camerman:* Denis Lenoir. *Assistant soundman:* Bernard Leroux. *Make-up:* Ronaldo Ribeiro de Abreu. *Script-girl:* Sandra Coelho de Souza. *Assistant directors:* Alain Centonze, Chantal Nicole, Michel Champetier. *Still photography:* Muriel Bonnet. *Executive producer:* Pierre-Henri Deleau. *Head of production:* Hubert Niogret. *Producer:* Jean-Daniel Pollet; *co-producer:* Vincent Malle. *Incidental music:* sonata by François Couperin; *"Soneto de Spinoza"* by Jorge Luis Borges *with music by* Hugo Santiago; *"El muelle,"* composed by Miguel Abuelo; *pop group:* Hijos de Nada. *Cast:* Patrice Dally (Spinoza), Noëlle Châtelet (Valérie), Daniel Vignat (Moreau), Roger Planchon (Alexis Artaxerxés), Bruno Devoldère (Mathieu/the journalist), Pierre Julien (Monsieur Marcel), Dominique Guezenec (Béatrice), Pierrette Destanque (Agnés), Maurice Born (Durtain), Jean-Daniel Pollet (Adam), Marc Monnet (Vidal). Also with Alain Aptekman, Luc Beraud, Jean-Jacques Beryl, Cathérine Binet, Federico de Cárdenas, Alain Colas, Pierre-André Cremieu, Jean-François Dion, Nicole Gasquet, Jim Hodgetts, Alain Jomy, Pela Mozart, Jacques Robert, Antoine Roblot, J.-J. Schakmundes, J.-J. Spoliansky, Henrik Stangerup, Stanislas Stanojevic, Robert Swaim, Juan Quirno. An Ilios Film-V. M. Productions-O.R.T.E. picture.

In the last lines of his review of *Dr. Jekyll and Mr. Hyde*, Borges conceived a hypothetical film that *Splits* brought into actuality: ". . . we may imagine a pantheistic film whose numerous characters finally resolve into One, who is everlasting." On the other hand, as that avant-garde that likes to call itself materialistic would have it, *Les Autres* is a film "that records within its text the process of its own production." The film presents an overture, a starter for the action, a rehearsal, even a clue that is obvious but also subtly inaccessible by reason of its placement. There are sudden breaks in the characters' erotic ecstasy as well as in the soundtrack's exultant music, fissures that confront the viewer with the spectacle of a film crew encircling, filming, and motivating a naked couple, fissures that reveal the sight of an orchestra recording those same harmonies which, up to that point, might have created a lofty, metaphysical illusion in purely sonorous terms. According to the director Hugo Santiago, "To present subjects that demand the genuine labor of decodification is even an ideological imperative" ("Introduction," *Les Autres* by Jorge Luis Borges, Adolfo Bioy Casares, Hugo Santiago; Paris, Christian Bourgois Editeur, 1974). But instead of fulfilling this proposition by stripping away the ingredients of fiction, *Les Autres* accumulates the outward signs of "cheap" fiction with exacting perversity: money lost in gambling, a masked ball where the fate of the guests is decided, love, death, intrigue. And, to the degree that this intrigue grows increasingly tangled, its twisted strands attenuate until the thing is a mere shadow of situations in novels, a sign for other signs that turn the loveliest images into reflections of the idea that summons and informs them. Again, according to Santiago: "A perfectly classic plot, clearly shaped with originality according to traditions that are part Anglo-Saxon, part Oriental; the 'final explanation' of the mysterious framework and its total clarification makes the plot fantastic as well. (Nevertheless, no direct symbols, no allegories: the fantastic as a means to cutting through reality in order to reach a different reality, the fantastic as an analogous operation: an itinerary, a chain of analogies.)"

Seldom has a film so attentive to the beauty of its images and sounds aimed so intently at an effect beyond those appearances, at their eventual confluences and disjunctions. The snow-white skin of an elusive woman, the harmless tricks of some magicians, the mechanism of the search that seemingly controls the plot are all tokens of another process, whisking their unruly, surface appearance out of sight in order to bring the audience face to face with another film—different, conceivable, realizable—that might begin by dissolving those fictitious identities of place and character that move through *Les Autres* merely to indicate an idea of cinema. In the interview already referred to, Santiago has expressed the point of his film clearly: " . . . not to try to 'disorder' the story by literary techniques and devices and reproduce this confusion on film, but, on the contrary, to view the story as a 'natural object' (like a face, a street, a noise) and treat it, modify it, by cinematographic means, in order to turn it into movie material."

If, sustained by its "imitation" of a popular genre, *Invasión* extracted a superfluous though genuine interest from that ironic relationship, then *Les Autres*, where Robert Louis Stevenson and *The Thousand and One Nights* are snatches from a scarcely recalled dream, denies the spectator any enjoyment, except for participating in an intellectual adventure whose lucid pleasures demand that he renounce any simpler pleasures.

LOS ORILLEROS and EL MUERTO / CACIQUE BANDERIA

LOS ORILLEROS (Men from the River Banks). Argentina, 1975. 90 minutes. *Director:* Ricardo Luna. *Based on an original story by* Jorge Luis Borges *and* Adolfo Bioy Casares; *adapted by* Ricardo Luna. *Photography (Eastmancolor):* Aníbal González Paz. *Music:* Sebastián Piana. *Editing:* Antonio Ripoll, Sergio Zottola. *Sets and costumes:* Ricardo Luna. *Sound:* Jorge Castronuovo. *Executive producer:* Curio Maggioli. *Cast:* Rodolfo Bebán (Eliseo Rojas), Alberto Argibay (Fermín Soriano), Franklin Caicedo (Luna), Milagros de la Vega (Tránsito Rojas), Oscar Ferrigno (Ponciano Silveira), Antonio Grimau (Julio Morales), María Leal (Ercilia Larramendi), Inda Ledesma (Rosa Villalba), Egle Martin (Florencia). An Alamo Film production.

EL MUERTO / CACIQUE BANDEIRA. (The Dead Man / Boss Bandeira). Argentina-Spain, 1975. 105 minutes. *Director:* Héctor Olivera. *Based on the story "The Dead Man" by* Jorge Luis Borges. *Screenplay:* Héctor Olivera, Fernando Ayala, *with the supervision of* Juan Carlos Onetti. *Photography (Eastmancolor):* Juan Carlos Desanzo. *Music:* Ariel Ramírez. *Sets:* Oscar Piruzanto *(interiors) and* Emilio Basaldúa *(exteriors)*. *Editing:* Carlos Julio Piaggio. *Sound:* Norberto Castronuovo. *Costumes:* Maria Julia Bertotto. *Producers:* Fernando Ayala, Héctor Olivera; *associate producer:* Luis Osvaldo Repetto. *Cast:* Thelma Biral (O'Reilly), Juan José Camero (Benjamín Otálora), Francisco Rabal (Azevedo Bandeira), José María Gutiérrez (the Colonel), Raul Lavié (Piru), Jorge Villalba (Mocho), Antonio Iranzo (Ulpiano Suárez), Noemí Laserre (the madam), Ricardo Trigo (card player). An Aries (Buenos Aires)-Impala (Spain) production.

Two documentary interviews with Borges were made in Argentina, primarily for showing on television: *Borges sobre Borges* (1975; 40 minutes), produced and directed by Carlos Gdansky Orgambide and Adolfo M. García Videla; *Borges para millones* (1978; footage adding up to several hours of projection time, of which a normal-length cut version is available) made by Ricardo Wulicher and Bernardo Kamin.

SPLITS

SPLITS. U.S.A., 1978. 30 minutes. *Director:* Leandro Katz. *Script:* Ted Castle, Lynn Anander, Leandro Katz, *based on "Emma Zunz"* by Jorge Luis Borges. *Photography:* Viktor Vondracek, Leandro Katz. *Editing:* Viktor Vondracek. *Music:* Joseph Hayden. *Technical Collaboration:* Millennium Film Workshop, Boris Bode, Bill Brand, B. B. Opticals. *Sound:* Nancy Meshkoff. *Produced with the assistance of* Claire Tankel, the New York City Department of Cultural Affairs, and a C.A.P.S. grant. *Cast:* Lynn Anander, Kathy Gales, John Levin. *16mm., color. (Screened in the John Gibson Gallery, New York, during an exhibition of works by Leandro Katz, from 25 November to 23 December 1978.)*

A film by a visual artist whose work has evolved toward the audio-visual, *Splits* might at first seem to "betray" Borges—at least in regard to his most frequently expressed political sympathies (which really were antipathies). In fact, *Splits* is profoundly faithful to Borges.

Splits divides its story into a series of narrative "gestures," overtures not shaped according to narrative criteria. It also divides the central character's voice-over between two female voices: Emma, who always speaks in the third person, and Muriel, who slips from third to first person. Also, by means of the split screen, the film divides its images into series that multiply the action—sometimes concurrently, sometimes consecutively—just as the voices overlap or follow one another.

All these divisions, however, attempt to establish evidence of an underlying unity, to resolve the identities of Emma and her victim into collective figures of the exploited and the exploiter. Emma's motive for revenge—established in the exposition only to be cancelled later—is here displaced by a ceremony in which those officiating vanish as individuals: "It was clear in her mind that there was no distinction between her personal loneliness and her political loneliness, between her day-after-day life and her ideas about being used by everyone as a token with no sense at all. . . ."

Like Borges's story, Katz's film culminates in Emma's killing her father's employer. But where Borges presents Emma's believable falsification in order to play with the notion of truth and the truth-like, Katz attempts a parallel reflection on the means of representation that allows him to stage his own fiction: "It was a seminal death, an homage to the death of imagination, to the dead cinema of cinema death . . . a rupture. . . ."

Based on an ideological analysis alien to but not incompatible with Borges's story, Katz's film coincides with both the writer's skeptical treatment of all forms of individuality and with a certain discreet pantheism by which Borges occasionally let an individual be other individuals or a mere actor in a plot whose scope he does not realize. In this instance, it is only a matter of hailing "the time when History liquidates the Masters. . . ." In the film's proposed reading of Emma Zunz's crime, it is also possible to discern a relationship between the artist/director and Borges's prestigious text, a relationship dispersed within a still larger text, which might be that of History itself. The originality and independence of Katz's endeavor resides, precisely, in his not having accepted the received meaning of the master's words, in his forcing them to yield a meaning that was unrecognized, or, at any rate, *other*.

GHAZAL, A INTRUSA, ORAINGOZ IZEN GABE

GHAZAL. Iran, 1975. 100 minutes color. *Director*: Massoud Kimia'i. *Screenplay based on "La intrusa"* by Jorge Luis Borges. *Photography*: Ne'mat Haqiqi. *Music*: Esfandiar Monfareezadeh. *Cast*: Mohamed Ali Fardin, Faramarz Qaribian, Pouri Bana'i. *An* Avant-Garde Cinema Group-Tel Film *production*.

A INTRUSA. Brazil, 1979. 100 minutes. *Director*: Carlos Hugo Christensen. *Screenplay*: Carlos Hugo Christensen, *based on the story "La intrusa"* by Jorge Luis Borges. *Dialogue*: Origenes Lesso, Ubirajara Raffo Constant. *Director of photography (Eastmancolor)*: Antonio Gonçalves. *Music*: Astor Piazzola. *Editor*: Rafael Justo. *Sets and costumes*: Ubirajara Raffo Constant. *Songs*: "Milonga de João Iberra" by Borges and Mário Barbará Dornelles; "Canção do Amanhecer" by Ubirajara Raffo Constant and Piazzola; "Baile de Rancho" by Thelma de Lima Freitas. *Singers*: Thelma de Lima Freitas, Mário Barbará, Jerónimo Martins. *Producer*: Carlos Hugo Christensen. *Cast*: Maria Zilda (Juliana), José de Abreu (Cristiano), Arlindo Barreto (Eduardo), Palmira Barbosa (Efigênia), Fernando de Almeida (João Iberra), Ricardo Wanick (Daniel Iberra), Mauricio Loyola (João dos Passaros), Heloisa Gedel (Young girl on the road), Nelson Pinto Bastos (Benito). *Released through* Embrafilme.

ORAINGOZ IZEN GABE / TODAVÍA SIN NOMBRE (Still Nameless). Spain, 1986. 58 minutes. *Director*: José J. Bakedano. *Screenplay*: Bernardo Atxaga, *based, uncredited, on the story "La intrusa"* by Jorge Luis Borges. *Director of photography (Eastmancolor)*: Gabriel Beristain. *Music*: Ruper Ordorika, Anton Valverde. *Editor*: José Luis Berlanga. *Sound*: José Luis Zabala. *Producer*: José J. Bakedano. *Cast*: Felix Arcarzo (Manuel), Juan Antonio Landaluze (Ramon), Elene Lizarralde (Esther), Eguzki, Luis Iriondo, Eskarne Aroma.

I have not been able to see the Iranian version of "La intrusa" ("The Intruder"), but the latter two curiosities, widely different in their cultural ambitions, testify to the unfathomable diversity of traces of Borges in filmmakers.

The hour-long Basque film partly results from the recent Spanish policy of cultural decentralization, which allows different regions not only to speak their own tongues but also to develop their cultural heritages. A very "minimal" venture, in which Borges's story goes uncredited, the film is intriguing for having both brothers run a greenhouse business, thus placing them in a latter-day professional context while keeping them isolated and close to nature. They speak Basque between themselves; the woman, a whore from the next town, speaks Spanish.

Speech is also the most interesting feature in the version of "La intrusa" made by a veteran Argentine director, active in Brazil for over thirty years by now. The accents of Rio Grande do Sul—bringing Brazilian Portuguese closer to Argentine Spanish, with the odd word of Spanish for aspects of everyday life and work on the plains—add a whiff of interest to this dismaying attempt at a dignified soft-core reading of the Borges story, whose homosexual subtext is ludicrously enhanced: at one point in their very academic "threesomes," both brothers, made-up and shampooed as if for a wild-life cigarette ad, brutally push aside the woman to go about their own business.

Lumen Books

Dialogue in the Void: Beckett and Giacometti
Matti Megged
ISBN: 0-9930829-01-8, $7.95

Culture and Politics in Nicaragua:
Testimonies of Poets and Writers
Steven White

Under a Mantle of Stars
A Play in Two Acts
Manuel Puig
Translated by Ronald Christ
ISBN: 0-930829-00-X, $6.95

Space in Motion
Juan Goytisolo
Translated by Helen Lane
ISBN: 0-930829-03-4, $8.95

Sor Juana's Dream
Luis Harss
ISBN: 0-930829-07-7, $9.95

For an Architecture of Reality
Michael Benedikt
ISBN: 0-930829-05-0, $9.95

Reverse Thunder
A Dramatic Poem
Diane Ackerman
ISBN: 0-930829-09-3, $7.95

Angst Cartography
Moji Baratloo & Clif Balch
ISBN: 0-930829-10-7, $8.95

M